Heirloom Afghans
to Knit & Crochet

Jean Leinhauser & Rita Weiss

Sterling Publishing Co., Inc.
New York

Library of Congress Cataloging-in-Publication Data

10 9 8 7 6 5 4 3 2 1

Published by Sterling Publishing Co., Inc.
387 Park Avenue South, New York, NY 10016
© 2005 by The Creative Partners, LLC™
Distributed in Canada by Sterling Publishing
c/o Canadian Manda Group, 165 Dufferin Street
Toronto, Ontario, Canada M6K 3H6
Distributed in Great Britain by Chrysalis Books Group
PLC The Chrysalis Building, Bramley Road, London
W10 6SP, England
Distributed in Australia by Capricorn Link (Australia)
Pty. Ltd. P.O. Box 704, Windsor, NSW 2756, Australia

Printed in China
All rights reserved

Sterling ISBN 1-4027-2305-9

For information about custom editions, special sales,
premium and corporate purchases, please contact
Sterling Special Sales Department at 800-805-5489 or
specialsales@sterlingpub.com.

Technical Editor: Susan Lowman
Photography: Carol Wilson Mansfield
Book Design: Graphic Solutions, inc-chgo
Produced by: Creative Partners,™ LLC.

The authors extend their thanks and appreciation
to these contributing designers:

Julia Bryant, Toronto, Canada
Nazanin S. Fard, Novato, California
Cynthia Grosch, Unionville, Connecticut
Janie Herrin, Jacksonville, Florida
Sheila Jones, Port Orchard, Washington
Jodi Lewanda, Farmington, Connecticut
Ruthie Marks, Ojai, California
Bonnie Pierce, Vancouver, Washington
Mary Jane Protus, Schenectady, New York
Linda Taylor, North Attleboro, Massachusetts
Margret Willson, Salt Lake City, Utah

A special note of thanks to Kathleen Sams and her associates
at Coats and Clark and to Catherine Blythe and the design
department at Patons Yarns for sharing many of their most
creative designs with us.

The afghans in this book were tested to ensure accuracy
and clarity of the instructions. We are grateful to the following
pattern testers:

Emma Blair, Chittenango, New York
Kimberly Britt, Gurnee, Illinois
Linda Bushey, Aquanga, California
Carrie Cristiano, Escondido, California
James Davis, Jacksonville, Florida
Kristen Ford, Portland, Oregon
Eileen Gaffigan, Silver Spring, Maryland
Patricia Honaker, East Liverpool, Ohio
Debra Hughes, Lusby, Maryland
Diane Limoges, Fordyce, Nebraska
Terry Morris, El Dorado Hills, California
Jane Rimmer, Palmyra, Pennsylvania
Kelly Robinson, Anza, California
Marjorie Scensny, Schaumburg, Illinois
Marsha Seiber, Sweet Home, Oregon

Wherever we have used a special yarn we have given the brand
name. If you are unable to find these yarns locally, write to the
following manufacturers who will be able to tell you where to
purchase their products, or consult their internet sites. We also
wish to thank these companies for supplying yarn for this book.

Bernat Yarns
320 Livingston Avenue South
Listowel, Ontario
Canada N4W 3H3
www.bernat.com

Caron International
Customer Service
P. O. Box 222
Washington, North Carolina 27889
www.caron.com

Knit One, Crochet Too, Inc
91 Tandberg Trail, Unit 6
Windham, Maine 04062
www.knitonecrochettoo.com

Lion Brand Yarn
34 West 15th Street
New York, New York 10011
www.LionBrand.com

Patons Yarns
2700 Dufferin St,
Toronto, Ontario
Canada M6B 4J3
www.patonsyarns.com

Plymouth Yarn Co., Inc.
500 Lafayette Street
P. O. Box 29
Bristol, Pennsylvania 19007-0028
www.plymouthyarn.com

Red Heart Yarns
Coats and Clark
Consumer Services
P. O. Box 12229
Greenville, South Carolina 29612-0229

Reynolds Yarns, a division of JCA
35 Scales Lane
Townsend, MA 01469-1011

TLC Yarns
Coats and Clark
Consumer Services
P. O. Box 12229
Greenville, South Carolina 29612

Introduction

Your sister will soon have a baby, the first grandchild in your family. You want to make something that will become an heirloom.

Your very best friend will soon celebrate her 30th birthday. You want to acknowledge this not very welcome milestone with a wonderful gift.

Your favorite aunt and uncle have a 50th wedding anniversary celebration in the near future. What can you give them to celebrate the achievement?

The answers to these gift-giving quandaries lie in this book.

Whether you knit or crochet, or both, you will find the perfect afghan design here that will say you care in a very personal way because these are all luxurious afghans intended for those special people in your life.

Because you want to make something that will always be treasured, you may wish to use a special yarn such as cashmere, or silk or mohair to craft your gift. Or you may prefer to choose an intricate design that will challenge you, but will show off your talents. The afghans in this collection were chosen because they fit the description of a luxurious gift for a special person.

And you don't have to use these fabulous designs only for gifts – it's all right to make one just for yourself!

Table of Contents

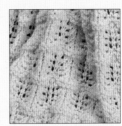
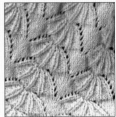

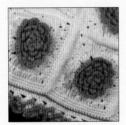

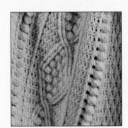

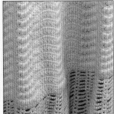

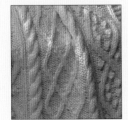

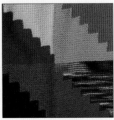

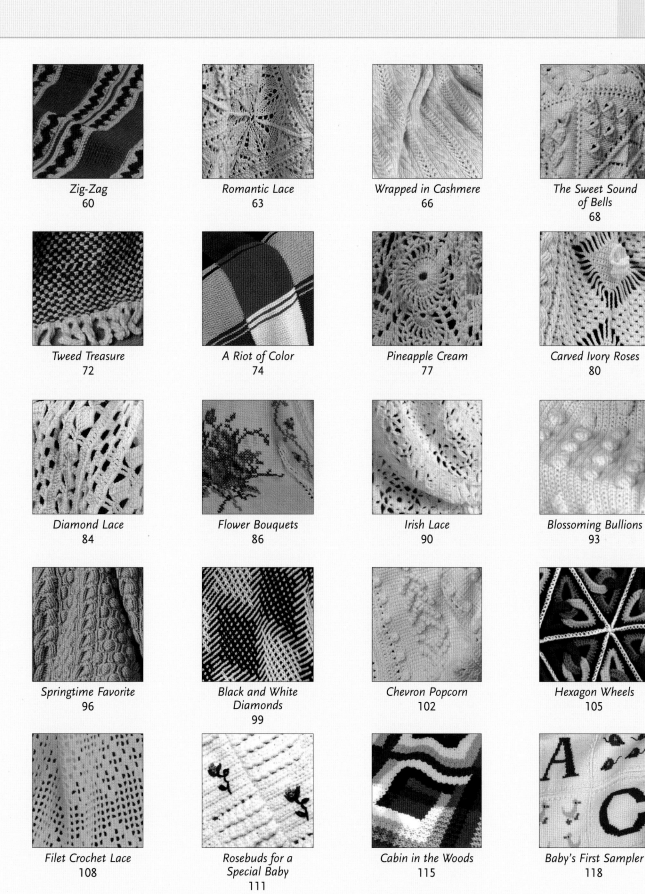

Sweetly feminine, this charming afghan will bring happy smiles to anyone who surrounds herself with its beauty. Work it in the favorite colors or decorating colorway of the fortunate future recipient.

Rosy Outlook

SIZE
52" x 67"

MATERIALS
Worsted Weight Yarn,
   18 oz dark rose (A)
   16 oz light pink (B)
   5 oz white (C)
Note: *Photographed model made with TLC® Lustre™ #5730 Coral Rose (A), #5718 Light Pink, and #5001 White*
Size 9 (5.5 mm) knitting needles (or size required for gauge)

GAUGE
14 sts= 3" in patt
20 rows= 4" in patt

SCALLOP PATTERN

Row 1 (right side): K1; * YO, K3, P2, P3tog, P2, K3, YO, K1; rep from * across.

Row 2: P1; *P4, K5, P5; rep from * across.

Row 3: K1; *YO, K4, P1, P3tog, P1, K4, YO, K1; rep from * across.

Row 4: P1; *P5, K3, P6; rep from * across.

Row 5: K1; *YO, K5, P3tog, K5, YO, K1; rep from * across.

Row 6: P1, *P6, K1, P7; rep from * across.

Rep Rows 1 through 6 for pattern.

Instructions

Panel 1 (make 3)
With A, CO 43 sts. Work patt Rows 1 through 6 until panel measures 67" from CO row, ending by working Row 5. BO loosely in knit.

Panel 2 (make 4)
With B, CO 29 sts. Work patt Rows 1 through 6 until panel measures 67" from CO row, ending by working Row 5. BO loosely in knit.

Panel 3 (make 2)
With C, CO 15 sts. Work patt Rows 1 through 6 until panel measures 67" from CO row, ending by working Row 5. BO loosely in knit.

Joining
Taking care to have all BO edges at top, sew panels tog in this order, from left to right:

   Panel 1

   Panel 2

   Panel 3

   Panel 2

   Panel 1 (center panel)

   Panel 2

   Panel 3

   Panel 2

   Panel 1

A traditional fisherman afghan gets an updated look with dimensional rows of flowers and leaves, artfully created in yarn. Cables and bobbles also provide textured accents in this unusual afghan. Wherever it is displayed, it is sure to become a conversation piece.

knit
Fisherman Flowers

Designed by Rita Weiss

SIZE
45" x 61"

MATERIALS
Worsted weight yarn,
 36 oz cream
*Note: Photographed model made with TLC® Essentials™
 #2313 Aran*
Size 10 (6 mm) knitting needles (or size required
 for gauge)
Cable needle

GAUGE
7 sts = 2" in Stockinette Stitch (knit one row,
 purl one row)

STITCH GUIDE

Cable Back (CB): Sl next 2 sts onto cable needle and
hold in back of work, K2, then K2 from cable needle:
CB made.

Twist Left (TL): Sl next 2 sts onto cable needle and
hold in front of work. P2, then K2 from cable needle:
TL made.

Twist Right (TR): Sl next 2 sts onto cable needle and
hold in back of work. K2, then P2 from cable needle:
TR made.

Popcorn (PC): Work (P1, K1) twice in next st; lift 2nd,
3rd and 4th sts at tip of right-hand needle over first
st: PC made.

Cable Twist (CT): Sl next 3 sts to cable needle, hold
in back of work; K3, then K3 from cable needle; sl next
3 stitches to cable needle, hold in front of work; K3,
then K3 from cable needle: CT made.

Bobble(B): Work into next st as follows: K1, (YO, K1)
3 times: 7 lps on needle; lift all sts, one by one over last
worked st, beg with 2nd from last (one st remaining).
Sl last st back to left-hand needle and K1: Bobble made.

*Note: Always slip stitches as to knit; keep yarn in back of
slipped stitch.*

Instructions

Panel A (make 2)
CO 20 sts.

Knit 4 rows, then begin patt.

Row 1 (right side): K1, P1, K1, P3; *sl 1 as to knit, K2,
PSSO 2 knit sts, P2; rep from* to last 4 sts, (P1, K1)
twice

Row 2 (wrong side): K1, P1, K1, K3; *P1, YO, P1, K2;
rep from * to last 4 sts, K2, P1, K1.

Row 3: K1, P1, K1, P3; *K3 (work the YO of prev row
as a st), P2; rep from * to last 4 sts, (P1, K1) twice

Row 4: K1, P1, K1, K3; *P3, K2; rep from * to last 4 sts,
K2, P1, K1.

Rep Rows 1 through 4 for patt until panel measures
about 60" ending by working a Row 2. Knit 4 rows.
BO loosely in knit. Weave in all ends.

Panel B (make 4)
CO 20 sts.

Knit 4 rows, then begin patt.

Row 1 (right side): K1, P1, sl 1, P1, K12, P1, sl 1,
P1, K1.

Row 2 (wrong side): (P1, K1) twice, P12, (K1, P1)
twice.

Rows 3 through 8: Rep Rows 1 and 2.

Row 9: K1, P1, sl 1, P1, CT over next 12 sts, P1, sl 1,
P1, K1.

Row 10: (P1, K1) twice, P12, (K1, P1) twice.

Rows 11 through 24: Rep Rows 1 and 2.

Rows 25 and 26: Rep Rows 9 and 10.

Rows 27 through 32: Rep Rows 1 and 2.

Rows 33 and 34: Rep Rows 9 and 10.

Rep Rows 1 through 34 for patt until panel measures about 60", ending by working a wrong-side row. Knit 4 rows. Bind off loosely in knit. Weave in all ends.

Panel C (make 2)

Cast on 27 sts.

Knit 4 rows, then begin patt.

Row 1(right side): K1, P1, sl 1, P1, K5, P2, K2, P1, K2, P2, K5, P1, sl 1, P1, K1.

Row 2 (wrong side): (P1, K1) twice, P4, K3, P2, K1, P2, K3, P4, (K1, P1) twice.

Row 3: K1, P1, sl 1, P1, K4, P2, K2tog, K1, YRN, P1, YO, K1, sl 1, K1, PSSO, P2, K4, P1, sl 1, P1, K1.

Row 4: (P1, K1) twice, P3, K3, P3, K1, P3, K3, P3, (K1, P1) twice.

Row 5: K1, P1, sl 1, P1, K3, P2, K2tog, K1, YO, K1, P1, K1, YO, K1, sl 1, K1, PSSO, P2, K3, P1, sl 1, P1, K1.

Row 6: (P1, K1) twice, P2, K3, P4, K1, P4, K3, P2, (K1, P1) twice.

Row 7: K1, P1, sl 1, P1, K2, P2, K2tog, K1, YO, K2, P1, K2, YO, K1, sl 1, K1, PSSO, P2, K2, P1, sl 1, P1, K1.

Row 8: (P1, K1) twice, P1, K3, P5, K1, P5, K3, P1, (K1, P1) twice.

Row 9: K1, P1, sl 1, P1, K1, P2, K2tog, K1, YO, K3, P1, K3, YO, K1, sl 1, K1, PSSO, P2, K1, P1, sl 1, P1, K1.

Row 10: (P1, K1) twice, K3, P6, K1, P6, K3, (K1, P1) twice.

Row 11: K1, P1, sl 1, P1, P2, (K2tog, K1, YO, K1) twice, YO, K1, sl 1, K1, PSSO, K1, YO, K1, sl 1, K1, PSSO, P2, P1, sl 1, P1, K1.

Row 12: (P1, K1) twice, K2, P6, K1, P1, K1, P6, K2, (K1, P1) twice.

Row 13: K1, P1, sl 1, P1, P2, K3, K2tog, K1, YRN, P1, K1, P1, YO, K1, sl 1, K1, PSSO, K3, P2, P1, sl 1, P1, K1.

Row 14: (P1, K1) twice, K2, P5, K2, P1, K2, P5, K2 (K1, P1) twice.

Row 15: K1, P1, sl 1, P1, P2, K2, K2tog, K1, YRN, P2, K1, P2, YO, K1, sl 1, K1, PSSO, K2, P2, P1, sl 1, P1, K1.

Row 16: (P1, K1) twice, K2, P4, K3, P1, K3, P4, K2, (K1, P1) twice.

Row 17: K1, P1, sl 1, P1, P2, K1, K2tog, K1, YRN, P3, K1, P3, YO, K1, sl 1, K1, PSSO, K1, P2, P1, sl 1, P1, K1.

Row 18: (P1, K1) twice, K2, P3, K4, P1, K4, P3, K2, (K1, P1) twice.

Row 19: K1, P1, sl 1, P1, P2, K2 tog, K1, YRN, P3, B, P1, B, P3, YO, K1, sl 1, K1, PSSO, P2, P1, sl 1, P1, K1.

Row 20: (P1, K1) twice, K2, P1, K13, P1, K2, (K1, P1) twice.

Row 21: K1, P1, sl 1, P1, P6, B, P5, B, P6, P1, sl 1, P1, K1.

Row 22: (P1, K1) twice, P1, K17, P1, (K1, P1) twice.

Row 23: K1, P1, sl 1, P1, K3, P2, B, P1, P2tog, YRN, P2tog, YRN, P2, B, P2, K3, P1, sl 1, P1, K1.

Row 24: (P1, K1) twice, P3, K13, P3, (K1, P1) twice.

Row 25: K1, P1, sl 1, P1, K3, P2, B, (P2 tog, YRN) 3 times, P1, B, P2, K3, P1, sl 1, P1, K1.

Row 26: Rep Row 24.

Row 27: K1, P1, sl 1, P1, K3, P2, B, P1, (P2tog, YRN) twice, P2, B, P2, K3, P1, sl 1, P1, K1.

Row 28: Rep Row 24.

Row 29: K1, P1, sl 1, P1, K4, P2, B, P5, B, P2, K4, P1, sl 1, P1, K1.

Row 30: (P1, K1) twice, P4, K11, P4, (K1, P1) twice.

Row 31: K1, P1, sl 1, P1, K6, P2, B, P1, B, P2, K6, P1, sl 1, P1, K1.

Row 32: (P1, K1) twice, P7, K5, P7, (K1, P1) twice.

Row 33: K1, P1, sl 1, P1, K8, P3, K8, P1, sl 1, P1, K1.

Row 34: (P1, K1) twice, P 19, (K1, P1) twice.

Rep Rows 1 through 34 for patt until panel measures about 60", ending by working a wrong-side row. Where necessary, push bobbles through to right side. Knit 4 rows. BO loosely in knit. Weave in all ends.

Panel D (make 1)

Cast on 52 sts.

Knit 4 rows, then begin patt.

Row 1 (right side): P2, (K2, P8, CB, P8, K2) twice, P2.

Row 2 (wrong side): K2, (P2, K8, P4, K8, P2) twice, K2.

Row 3: P2, (TL, P4, TR, TL, P4, TR) twice, P2.

Row 4: K4, (P2, K4) 8 times.

Row 5: P4, (TL, TR, P4) 4 times.

Row 6: K6, (P4, K8) 3 times; P4, K6.

Row 7: P6; *CB, P3 (PC) twice, P3 ; rep from * twice more, CB, P6.

Row 8: K6, (P4, K8) 3 times; P4, K6.

Row 9: P4, (TR, TL, P4) 4 times.

Row 10: K4, (P2, K4) 8 times.

Row 11: P2, (TR, P4, TL) 4 times, P2.

Row 12: K2, P2, (K8, P4) 3 times, K8, P2, K2.

Row 13: P2, K2, *P3, (PC) twice, P3, CB; rep from * twice, P3, (PC) twice, P3, K2, P2.

Row 14: Rep Row 12.

Rep rows 1 through 14 for patt until panel measures about 60" ending by working a wrong-side row. Knit 4 rows. Bind off loosely in knit. Weave in all ends.

Joining

Hold a Panel A and a Panel B with right sides tog; sew tog with overcast st, carefully matching rows.

Following diagram, join rem panels in the same manner.

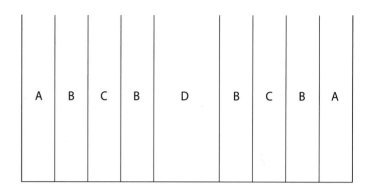

Fringe

Following Fringe Instructions on page 127, make triple knot fringe. Cut 26" strands of yarn; use 8 strands for each knot fringe. Tie knots evenly spaced (about every 5th st) across short end of afghan. Then work triple knot fringe following instructions. Trim ends evenly.

Open work and textured stitches are combined here for a light and lovely look. It looks complicated, but is really quick and easy to make. It's made in an off-white yarn to showcase the dimensional stitches and will blend in beautifully in any setting.

knit
Perfect in White

SIZE
45" x 61"

MATERIALS
Worsted weight yarn,
  37 oz off white
Note: *Photographed model made with Red Heart® Super
  Saver® #313 Aran*
36" Size 9 (5.5 mm) circular knitting needle (or size
  required for gauge)

GAUGE
22 sts = 4³/4" in pattern
12 rows= 2¹/4"

STITCH GUIDE

SSK = Sl next 2 sts as if to knit, one at a time, to right
needle, then insert point of left needle into fronts of
these 2 sts and knit them tog.

Instructions

CO 211 sts; do not join; work back and forth in rows.

Row 1 (right side): Knit.

Row 2: Knit.

Row 3: K1; *(K2tog) twice, (YO, K1) 3 times, YO,
(SSK) twice; rep from * to last st, K1.

Row 4: Purl.

Rows 5 through 10: Rep Rows 3 and 4 three more
times.

Rows 11 and 12: Knit.

Rep Rows 1 through 12 until piece measures 61" from
beginning.

Next Row: Knit.

BO. Weave in ends.

Richly textured, this elegant design is this is a perfect gift for a knitter friend who will appreciate the lovely design and the intricate workmanship that created it. The bear claw motif is a knitting classic, and is used here very effectively.

knit
Bear Claw Throw

Designed by Rita Weiss for Coats & Clark

SIZE
44" x 60"

MATERIALS
Worsted weight yarn,
  26 oz cream
Note: *Photographed model made with TLC® Amoré™*
  # 3103 Vanilla.
36" size 8 (5 mm) circular knitting needle (or size
  required for gauge)

GAUGE
18 sts = 4 in garter st (knit each row)

Instructions
CO 152 sts. Do not join; work back and forth in rows.

Lower Border
Rows 1 through 6: Knit.

Center

Row 1 (right side): K4; *K1, YO, (K1, P3) 4 times, K1, YO; rep from * to last 4 sts, K4: 168 sts.

Row 2: K4; *P2, (K3, P1) 4 times, P2; rep from * to last 4 sts, K4.

Row 3: K4; *K2, YO, (K1, P3) 4 times, K1, YO, K1; rep from * to last 4 sts, K4: 184 sts.

Row 4: K4; *P3, (K3, P1) 4 times, P3; rep from * to last 4 sts, K4.

Row 5: K4; *K3, YO, (K1, P3) 4 times, K1, YO, K2; rep from * to last 4 sts, K4: 200 sts.

Row 6: K4; *P4, (K3, P1) 4 times, P4; rep from * to last 4 sts, K4.

Row 7: K4; *K4, YO, (K1, P2tog, P1) 4 times, K1, YO, K3; rep from * to last 4 sts, K4: 184 sts.

Row 8: K4; *P5, (K2, P1) 4 times, P5; rep from * to last 4 sts, K4.

Row 9: K4; *K5, YO, (K1, P2tog) 4 times, K1, YO, K4; rep from * to last 4 sts, K4: 168 sts.

Row 10: K4; *P6, (K1, P1) 4 times, P6; rep from * to last 4 sts, K4.

Row 11: K4; *K6, YO, (sl 1, K1, PSSO) 4 times, K1, YO, K5; rep from * to last 4 sts, K4: 152 sts.

Row 12: K4, P to last 4 sts, K4.

Rep Rows 1 through 12 until afghan measures about 59" from beg, ending by working a Row 11.

Top Border
Rows 1 through 6: Knit.

BO loosely in knit.

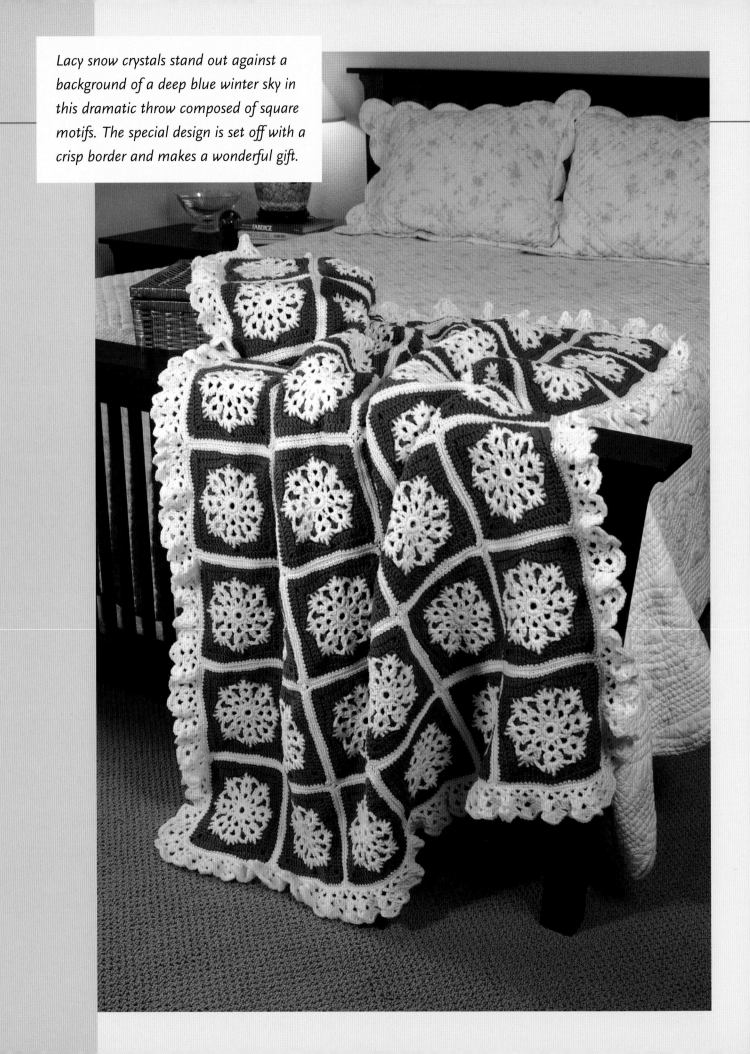

Lacy snow crystals stand out against a background of a deep blue winter sky in this dramatic throw composed of square motifs. The special design is set off with a crisp border and makes a wonderful gift.

crochet
Snowfleck Throw

Designed by Janie Herrin

SIZE
42" x 56" before border

MATERIALS
Worsted weight yarn,
   30 oz white
   22 oz blue
*Note: Photographed model made with Red Heart®
   Super Saver® #0311 White and #0886 Blue*
Size G (4 mm) crochet hook (or size required
   for gauge)

GAUGE
One square = 7" x 7"

Instructions

Square (make 48)
With white ch 7, join with sl st to form a ring.

Rnd 1: Ch 1, 16 sc in ring, join with sl st in beg sc.

Rnd 2: Ch 6, (counts as first dc and ch-3), dc in
same st; *skip next st, in next st work (dc, ch 3, dc);
rep from * around, join with sl st in 3rd ch of beg
ch-6: 8 ch-3 sps.

Rnd 3: Sl st in next ch-3 sp, ch 3, (dc, ch 3, 2 dc) in
same sp; *in next ch-3 sp work (2 dc, ch 3, 2 dc); rep
from * around, join in 3rd ch of ch-3.

Rnd 4: Sl st into next ch-3 sp, ch 3, (2 dc, ch 2, 3 dc)
in same sp, ch 1; *in next ch-3 sp, work (3 dc, ch 2,
3 dc), ch 1; rep from * around, join, finish off white:
8 ch-2 sps.

Rnd 5: Join blue with sc in any ch-2 sp, 2 more sc in
same sp; *in next 3-dc group work sc in sp between
first 2 dc, sc in sp between middle and last dc of same
3-dc group; reaching hook behind next ch-1 sp, work
2 tr in center sp between 4 dc group 2 rows below;
work sc in each sp of next 3-dc group as before **,
work 3 sc in next ch-2 sp; rep from * 6 times more,
then rep from * to ** once; join with sl st in beg sc.

Rnd 6: Ch 3; *in next sc, work (2 dc, ch 2, 2 dc): corner made; dc in next 5 sts, hdc in next 2 sc, skip next
sc, sl st in next sc, skip next sc, hdc in next 2 sc; ** dc
in next 5 sts; rep from * 2 times more, then rep from
* to ** once, dc in next 4 sts, join; 4 ch-2 corner sps.

Rnd 7: Ch 3, dc in next 2 dc; * in next ch-2 sp work
corner, dc in next 6 sts, sc in next 7 sts, ** dc in next 6
sts; rep from * 2 times more, then rep from * to ** once,
dc in next 3 dc, join, finish off blue.

Rnd 8: Join white with sc in any ch-2 corner sp, 2 sc in
same sp; *sc in next 23 sts, 3 sc in next ch-2 corner sp;
rep from * around ending with sc in last 23 sts, join,
finish off, weave in ends.

Joining
Join squares in 6 rows of 8 squares each. To join, hold
2 squares with right sides together. Carefully matching
sts, with white, sew tog along one side, beginning in
center sc of one corner and ending in center sc of next
corner. Continue to join in rows, then sew rows
together in same manner.

Border
Rnd 1: Hold afghan with right side facing and one
short end at top. Join white with sc in center sc of 3-sc
corner group, 2 sc in same st; sc evenly around edges,
working 3 sc in center sc at each corner and adjusting
sts to keep work flat; join with sl st in beg sc; sl st in
next sc (corner sc of beg 3-sc group).

Rnd 2: Ch 6 (counts as first dc and ch-3), dc in same
st; *skip 2 sc, in next sc work (dc, ch 3, dc); rep from
* around having (dc, ch 3, dc) in center sc of each 3-sc
corner group; join with slip st to 3rd ch of beg ch-6.

Rnd 3: Rep Rnd 3 of Square instructions.

Rnd 4: Rep Rnd 4 of Square instructions.

Finish off; weave in ends.

The stark black and white combination with deep fringe makes a perfect accent for a contemporary room. Give this afghan to your most sophisticated friend and be prepared for compliments galore. It would be a great gift for a man, too.

crochet
Sophistication

designed by Janie Herrin

SIZE
51" x 59"

MATERIALS
Worsted weight yarn,
  21 oz black
  18 oz white
Bulky weight yarn,
  11 oz black and white blend
Note: *Photographed model made with Red Heart®*
  Classic® # 12 black , # 1white and Casual Cot'n™
  #3550 zebra
Size I (5.5 mm) crochet hook (or size required for gauge)

GAUGE
3 dc = 1" with worsted weight yarn
9-rnd square = 8½"

STITCH GUIDE

Beginning Cluster (beg CL): Ch 2, holding back last lp of each dc, work 2 dc in same sp, YO, draw thru all 3 lps on hook: beg CL made

Cluster (CL): Holding back last lp of each dc, work 3 dc in sp indicated, YO, draw thru all 4 lps on hook: CL

Instructions

Square (make 42)
With bulky yarn , ch 5, join with sl st to form a ring.

Rnd 1: Ch 1, 12 sc in ring, join in first sc.

Rnd 2: Ch 1, sc in same sc; *ch 2, sc in next sc; rep from * around, ending ch 2; join in beg sc: 12 ch-2 sps.

Rnd 3: Sl st in next ch-2 sp, work beg CL, ch 3, CL in same sp; *ch 3, skip next sp, in next sp work (CL , ch 3, CL); rep from * around ending, with ch 3, join in top of beg CL: 12 CL; finish off bulky yarn.

Rnd 4: Join white yarn with sl st in next ch-3 sp, ch 3 (equals first dc), 4 dc in same sp; *ch 3, sc in next sp, ch 3, 5 dc in next sp; rep from * around, ending with sl st in

beg dc; ch 3, pull up lp and drop yarn, do not cut yarn.

Rnd 5: Join black yarn with sc in first dc of any 5-dc group; *(ch 2, skip next dc, sc in next dc) twice, (ch 2, sc in next sp) twice, ch 2, sc in next dc; rep from * around ending with sl st in beg sc: 30 ch-2 sps.

Rnd 6: Sl st in next ch-2 sp, ch 1, 2 sc in same sp; 2 sc in each sp around, join in beg sc: 60 sc; finish off black yarn.

Rnd 7: Pick up white yarn from Row 4, sl st in nearest sc, ch 4, in same st work (tr, ch 2, 2 tr); *ch 2, skip 2 sc, 2 dc in next sc; (ch 2, skip 2 sc, 2 sc in next sc) twice; ch 2, skip 2 sc, 2 dc in next sc; ch 2, skip 2 sc, in next sc work (2 tr, ch 2, 2 tr); rep from * around, ending with ch 2, sl st in top of beg ch-4: 24 ch-2 sps.

Rnd 8: Ch 1, sc in same st, sc in next tr; *3 sc in ch-2 corner sp, sc in each of next 2 tr, (2 sc in sp, sc in each of next 2 sts) 5 times; rep from * around, ending with 2 sc in last sp; join in beg sc, finish off.

Rnd 9: Join black in center sc of any 3-sc corner group; in same sc work (ch 3, dc, ch 3, 2 dc) for corner; *dc in each sc to next 3-sc corner group, in center sc work (2 dc, ch 3, 2 dc; rep from * twice, dc in each rem dc, join in 3rd ch of beg ch-3. Finish off black.

Joining
Join squares with black yarn; to join, hold 2 squares with right sides tog and sew with overcast st along one side edge, carefully matching sts and corners. Join in 7 rows of 6 squares each.

Edging
With right side of work facing you, join black yarn in corner sp at top right; 3 sc in same sp, sc in each st around, adjusting sts as needed to keep work flat, and working 3 sc in each outer corner sp. Finish off.

Fringe
Following Fringe instructions on page 127 cut 18" strands from all three yarns. Work single knot fringe across each short end, spacing knots about 3 sts apart.

Choose this lovely afghan as a perfect gift for a cherished mother, an adored grandmother a perfect aunt, or any other special woman in your life. What a wonderful surprise it would be to commemorate a birthday, anniversary or Mother's Day.

Á La Foo-Foo

designed by Janie Herrin

SIZE
50" x 63"

MATERIALS
Worsted weight yarn,
  24 oz white
  8 oz pink
  18 oz green
Note: *Photographed model made with Red Heart®
Super Saver® #316 Soft White, #372 Rose Pink and
#661 Frosty Green*
Size I (5.5 mm) crochet hook (or size required
  for gauge)

GAUGE
12 dc = 4"
Square =12" x 12"

STITCH GUIDE

V-st: (dc, ch 2, dc) in st or sp indicated

Post sc (Psc): Insert hook from front to back to front
around post (vertical bar) of specified st, YO and draw
up a lp, YO and draw through 2 lps: Psc made.

Instructions

Square (make 20)

With white, ch 4; join with a sl st to form a ring.

Rnd 1 (right side): Ch 1, 8 sc in ring, join with sl st in
beg sc.

Rnd 2: Ch 1, sc in joining, ch 3, (sc in next sc, ch 3)
around, join in beg sc: 8 ch-3 sps.

Rnd 3: Sl st in next ch-3 sp, ch 1; in same sp and in
each sp around work (sc, hdc, dc, hdc, sc); join in beg
sc: 8 petals made.

Rnd 4: Ch 2, turn; working on wrong side, Psc around
sc on Rnd 2, ch 4; (Psc around next sc on Rnd 2, ch 4)
around, join: 8 ch-4 sps.

Rnd 5: Ch 1, turn; working on right side, in next ch-4
sp and in each sp around work (sc, hdc, 2 dc, hdc, sc),
end with sl st in beg sc, ch 1, pull up a long lp (to be
picked up later); drop yarn, do not cut.

Rnd 6: With right side facing, join pink with Psc
around any sc on Rnd 2, ch 3, (Psc around next sc,
ch 3) around, join: 8 ch-3 sps.

Rnd 7: Ch 3; *sc in first sc of next petal on Rnd 3,
ch 2, (sc in next st, ch 2) 3 times, sc in last sc of same
petal, dc in sc below on Rnd 6; rep from * around, end
with last sc, join in 3rd ch of beg ch-3.

Rnd 8: Ch 2, working around petals on Rnd 5, (sc,
ch 2) in each st around, join in beg sc; finish off.

Rnd 9: Pick up white dropped lp on Rnd 5, sc in ch-2
sp bet petals on Rnd 8, ch 4, skip 2 sps, sc in next sp
(you should be in center sp of petal); (ch 4, skip 2 sps,
sc in next sp) around, ch 4, join beg sc: 16 ch-4 sps.

Rnd 10: Sl st in next ch-4 sp, ch 3 (equals first dc),
4 dc in same sp; (5 dc in next sp) around; join, finish
off: 80 dc.

Rnd 11: With right side facing, join green with sl st in
first dc of any 5-dc group, ch 5, dc in same st; (ch 1,
skip 3 dc, work V-st in next dc) around, skip last 3 dc,
end with sc in 3rd ch of beg ch 5: 20 V-sts.

Rnd 12: Ch 5, dc in same sp, ch 1, (skip next V-st,
work V-st in sp before next V-st, ch 1) 3 times; *skip
next V-st, in sp before next V-st work (V-st, ch 2, V-st):
corner made; ch 1, (skip next V-st, work V-st in sp
before next V-st, ch 1) 4 times; rep from * around, skip
last V-st, work corner in sp before next V-st, ch 1, join
in 3rd ch of beg ch 5: 24 V-sts.

Rnd 13: Sl st in ch-2 sp of next V-st, ch 1, in same sp
work 3 sc, sc in ch-1 sp; (3 sc in ch-2 sp of next V-st, sc
in next ch-1 sp) 3 times; *3 hdc in ch-2 sp of next V-st,
in corner ch-2 sp work (3 dc, ch 2, 3 dc); 3 hdc in ch-2
sp of next V-st, sc in ch-1 sp, (3 sc in ch-2 sp of next V-

Á La Foo-Foo

st, sc in next ch-1 sp) 4 times; rep from * around, end with last 3 hdc, sc in ch-1 sp; join in beg sc, finish off: 68 sc, 24 hdc, 24 dc.

Rnd 14: Join white with sl st in any corner ch-2 sp, ch 5, (dc, ch 2, V-st) in same sp: beg corner made; *(ch 2, skip next 2 sts, dc in next st) 9 times, ch 2, skip next 2 sts, (V-st, ch 2, V-st) in corner; rep from * around, end with last ch 2; join to 3rd ch of beg ch 5: 52 ch-2 sps.

Rnd 15: Sl st in ch-2 sp of V-st, ch 4 (equals first dc plus ch 1); *work corner in corner sp, ch 1, dc in ch-2 sp of next V-st, ch 1, (skip next ch-2 sp, V-st in next dc) 9 times, ch 1, dc in ch-2 sp of next V-st, ch 1; rep from * around, end with last ch 1; join in beg dc; finish off: 44 V-sts, 8 dc.

Rnd 16: Join green with sl st in any corner ch-2 sp, ch 2 (equals first hdc), 2 hdc in same sp; *hdc in sp of next V-st, hdc in (ch-1 sp, in next dc and in next ch-1 sp); working across next 9 V-sts, hdc in each dc and in each ch-2 sp; hdc in (ch-1 sp, next dc, next ch-1 sp and in sp of next V-st), 3 hdc in corner sp; rep from * around ending with sl st in beg hdc; finish off; weave in ends.

Joining

With green, holding two squares with right sides facing, sew together with overcast stitch, working in outer loops only carefully matching stitches and corners. Make 4 strips of 5 squares each; then join strips in same manner.

Border

Hold afghan with right side facing and one short end at top. Join green with a sl st in outer corner st at top right.

Rnd 1: Ch 1, 3 sc in same st as joining; sc evenly around afghan, adjusting sts as needed to keep work flat, and working 3 sc in each rem outer corner; join with a sl st in beg sc; finish off green.

Rnd 2: Join white in center sc of any 3-sc corner group; ch 1, 3 sc in same sc; complete as for Rnd 1; join with sc tn beg sc.

Rnd 3: Sl st in next sc (center sc of 3-sc group), ch 1, in same st work (sc, ch 3, sc); *ch 3, skip next sc, sc in next sc; rep from * around working (sc, ch 3, sc) in rem center corner sts; end with last ch 3, join with sl st in beg sc; finish off, weave in all ends.

Knit
Woven-Look Blanket

Designed by Patons Design Staff

SIZE
Approx 49" x 56½"

MATERIALS
Worsted weight yarn,
   17½ oz dark purple (MC)
   14 oz red (A)
   14 oz blue (B)
   14 oz green (C)
Note: *Photographed model made with Patons® Décor*
   #1627 Rich Aubergine (MC), #1657 Claret (A), #1621
   Country Blue(B) and #1636 Sage Green (C)
29" Size 8 (5 mm) circular knitting needle (or size
   required for gauge)

GAUGE
17 sts = 4" in Seed St Patt
28 rows = 4"

STITCH GUIDE

Ridge Pattern
Row 1 (right side): Knit.

Row 2: Purl.

Row 3: Purl.

Row 4: Purl.

Row 5: Knit.

Row 6: Knit.

Rep Rows 1 through 6 for Ridge Pattern

Seed Stitch Pattern
Row 1 (right side): *K1, P1; rep from * to last st, K1.

Rep Row 1for Seed Stitch Pattern

Instructions

With MC, cast on 203 sts. ***Note:*** *Do not join; work back*
and forth in rows.

Foundation row (wrong side): Knit.

*With MC, work Ridge Patt for 32 rows, ending by
working Row 2 of Ridge Patt.**

With A, work 2 rows Seed St Patt.

With MC, work 2 rows Seed St Patt.

Rep last 4 rows twice more.

With A, work Ridge Patt for 32 rows, ending by working Row 2 of Ridge Patt.

With B, work 2 rows Seed St Patt.

With A, work 2 rows Seed St Patt.

Rep last 4 rows twice more.

With B, work Ridge Patt for 32 rows, ending by working Row 2 of Ridge Patt.

With C, work 2 rows Seed St Patt.

With B, work 2 rows Seed St Patt.

Rep last 4 rows twice more.

With C, work Ridge Patt for 32 rows ending by working Row 2 of Ridge Patt.

With MC, work 2 rows Seed St Patt.

With C, work 2 rows Seed St Patt.

Rep last 4 rows twice more.*

Rcp from * to * once more, then from * to **once.

With MC, BO.

Side edging

With right side of work facing and MC, pick up and
knit 257 sts evenly spaced along each side edge. Work
2 rows in Garter St (knit each row), ending by working
a right side row. BO.

Finish off.

It looks as if it came off the loom of an expert weaver – but it's really a fine example of the knitter's art . A striking combination of bold colors is worked into the unusual design. It's perfect piece to display in a den or home office setting.

Woven-Look Blanket

Fringe

Follow the instructions for Single Knot Fringe on page 127. Cut 14" lengths of yarn in all colors.

Taking 8 strands tog, knot into fringe across CO and BO edges in the following sequence:

(8 strands MC) twice
4 strands MC and 4 strands A
(8 strands A) twice
4 strands A and 4 strands B
(8 strands B) twice
4 strands B and 4 strands C
(8 strands C) twice
4 strands C and 4 strands MC.

Spectacular dimensional roses, which ramble across this striking afghan, are created by working bullion stitches. They may present a challenge to the crocheter but they are certain to be appreciated by the recipient of this magnificent afghan. As a final touch, a lovely double ruffle graces both ends of this lovely piece.

Promise Her A Rose Garden

designed by Bonnie Pierce
for the advanced crocheter

SIZE

35" x 49" before border

MATERIALS

Worsted weight yarn,
  29 oz white
  17 oz rose

Note: *Photographed model made with Red Heart® Super Saver® #311 White and #374 Country Rose*

Size H (5 mm) crochet hook (or size required for gauge)

GAUGE

square = 7" x 7"
7 sc = 2"

STITCH GUIDE

Bullion Stitch

If you've never used the bullion stitch before, you'll want to practice it before starting the afghan. It takes some practice to be able to do it easily, but once you've mastered bullions, you'll find them fun to work and will love the interesting texture they add to your projects. Bullions are worked like an hdc, but with a lot more yarn overs.

To practice the bullion stitch, work this sample swatch with scrap yarn:

With worsted weight scrap yarn, ch 11.

Row 1: Sc in 2nd ch from hook and in each rem ch: 10 sc; ch 2 (counts as first hdc of following row), turn.

Row 2: YO, insert hook in next sc and draw up a lp; YO and draw through all 3 lps on hook: one hdc made.

For the next st, YO twice, insert hook in next sc and draw up a lp; YO and draw through all 4 lps on hook. (**Fig 1**)

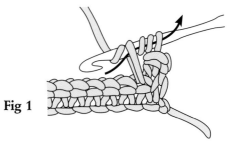

Fig 1

Try to draw the yarn through all 4 lps at once, but if necessary, you can use your fingers to pull the lps off one at a time: one 2-YO bullion st made.

For the next st, YO 3 times, insert hook in next sc and draw up a lp, YO and draw through all 5 lps at once; this will be a bit more difficult, but keep at it: one 3-YO bullion st made. (**Fig 2**)

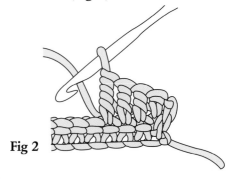

Fig 2

Continue in this manner across the row, adding one more YO at the beginning of each st, until you have 10 YOs. At end of row, ch 3, turn.

For the roses in this pattern, we use a 15-YO bullion, so continue working until you have mastered the stitch with 15 YOs in each. Take your time and pull the lps off by hand if necessary until you can do it in one sweeping motion.

Note: *When pattern specifies a bullion, that is a 15-YO bullion.*

Instructions

Square (make 35)

Center: With rose, ch 6, join with a sl st to form a ring.

Rnd 1: In ring work (ch 3, bullion, sl st) 5 times: 5 petals made; join with sl st in beg ch-3 sp.

Rnd 2: (Ch 3, bullion in same ch-3 sp of rnd below, sl st in next ch-3 sp) 5 times, join with sl st in beg ch-3 sp: 5 petals made.

Rnd 3: *Ch 4, (in same ch-3 sp work bullion, sl st, ch 4, bullion), sl st in next ch-3 sp; rep from * four times more, join in beg ch-3 sp: 10 petals made.

Rnd 4: Sl st in ch-4 sp, ch 1; (sc, hdc, 3 dc, hdc, sc) in same sp and in each ch-4 sp around; join in first sc.

Rnd 5: Working behind petal, (sl st around ch-4 sp of Rnd 3, ch 5) 10 times, join: 10 ch-5 sps. Finish off rose.

Rnd 6: Join white with sl st in any ch-5 sp, ch 3, 3 dc in same sp; 4 dc in each of the next 9 ch-5 sps, join: 40 dc.

Rnd 7: Ch 5 (counts as first dc and ch 2), work 3 dc in same joining for first corner, *dc in next 2 sts, hdc in next 2 sts, sc in next st, hdc in next 2 sts, dc in next 2 sts, (3 dc, ch 2, 3 dc) for corner in next st; rep from * around, ending last rep with dc in last 2 sts, work 2 dc at base of beg ch-5; join to 3rd ch of beg ch-5.

Rnd 8: Sl st into ch-2 sp, in same sp work Ch 5 (first dc and ch-2), work 2 dc in same sp for first corner, *(skip next st, 3 dc in next st, skip next st, dc in next 3 sts) twice; skip next st, 3 dc in next st, skip next st, (2 dc, ch2 2 dc) in ch-2 sp for corner; rep from * twice more, (skip next st, 3 dc in next st, skip next st, dc in next 3 sts) twice, skip next st, 3 dc in next st, dc at base of beg ch-5; join to 3rd ch of beg-5.

Rnd 9: Ch 1, sc in each st around, working 3 sc in each ch-2 corner sp; join, finish off, weave in ends.

Joining

To join squares, hold 2 squares with right sides facing and sew along one side with overcast st through outer lps only, carefully matching sts and corners.

Join in 7 rows of 5 squares each.

Border

Hold piece with right side facing and one short end at top.

Rnd 1: Join white with sc in outer corner center st at top right, 2 sc in same st; sc in each st around, working 3 sc in each rem corner and adjusting sts to keep work flat; join, finish off white.

Rnd 2: With rose, rep Rnd 1; finish off rose.

Rnd 3: With white, rep Rnd 1; finish off white. Weave in all ends.

Top Ruffle

Hold piece with wrong side facing and one short edge at top.

Row 1: Join white with sl st in center st of 3-sc corner group of outer corner at top right; ch 1, sc in same st; *ch 6, skip 3 sc, sc in next sc; rep from * across to next corner; ch 1, turn.

Row 2 (right side): Sc in first sc; *in next ch-6 sp work (sc, hdc, 3dc, hdc, sc): shell made; sc in next sc, rep from * across; ch 1, turn.

Row 3: Sc in first sc; *ch 7, sc in next sc between shells; rep from * across, ending with sc in last sc; ch 1, turn.

Row 4: Hdc in first sc; *in next ch-7 sp work (sc, hdc, 2 dc, tr, 2 dc, hdc, sc): shell made; hdc in next sc; rep from * across, finish off. Weave in ends.

Row 5: Hold piece with right side facing and join rose with sc in first hdc of Row 2; sc in each st across; finish off rose.

Row 6: With right side facing, join rose with sc in first hdc of Row 5; sc in each st across; finish off rose. Weave in all ends.

Bottom Ruffle

Hold piece with right side facing and opposite short end at top. Rep Rows 1 through 6 of Top Ruffle.

crochet
Pretty Pinwheels

Designed by Bonnie Pierce

SIZE
41" x 51"

MATERIALS
Worsted weight yarn,
- 18 oz white
- 14 oz blue
- 14 oz mauve

Note: Photographed model made with Bernat® Berella® "4" White #08942, Soft Periwinkle Blue #01143 and True Mauve #01306

Size E (3.5 mm) crochet hook (or size required for gauge)
Size G (4 mm) crochet hook (for edging)

GAUGE
8 dc = 2"
Square = 9½" x 9½"

STITCH GUIDE

Puff Stitch (Pst): With blue, (YO, insert hook in specified st and draw up a lp) 4 times, YO and draw through all 9 lps on hook; drop blue, ch 1 with white: Pst made

Instructions

Square (make 20)
With mauve and smaller hook, ch 8, join with a sl st to form a ring.

Rnd 1: Ch 1, 16 sc in ring; join with sl st in beg sc; finish off mauve.

Rnd 2: Join white with a sl st in any sc, ch 1, sc in same st; *ch 9, skip next st, sc in next st; rep from * 7 times more, join in first sc: 8 ch-9 sps.

Rnd 3: Ch 1, sc in same sc, * sc in next 4 chs, 3 sc in next ch, sc in next 4 chs, sc in next sc; rep from * 7 times more, ending last rep with sc in last 4 chs; join: 8 triangles.

Rnd 4: Ch 1, sc in same st; *working in back lps only, sc in next 5 sts, 3 sc in next st, sc in next 5 sts; working in both lps, sc in next sc; rep from * 7 times more, ending last rep with sc in last 5 sts; join.

Note: On Rnd 5, pull gently on carried blue as you work so it does not show through white sts.

Rnd 5: Ch 1, sc in same st; *working in back lps only, sc in next 2 sts; drop white, do not cut; Pst with blue in next st; working over blue, with white sc in next 3 sts, 3 sc in corner, sc in next 6 sts; working in both lps, sc in next sc; rep from * 7 times more, ending last rep with sc in last 6 sts; join; finish off blue.

Rnd 6: Ch 1, sc in same st; *working in back lps only, sc in next 2 sts, sc in top of Pst, (skip blue st), sc in next 4 sts, 3 sc in next st, sc in next 7 sts; working in both lps, sc in next st; rep from * 7 times more; ending last rep with sc in last 7 sts; join; finish off white.

Rnd 7: Join mauve with sl st in any sc between triangles, ch 1, sc in same st; *working in back lps only, sc in next 8 sts, 3 sc in next st, sc in next 8 sts; working in both lps, sc in next st; rep from * 7 times more, ending last rep with sc in last 8 sts; finish off mauve.

Rnd 8: Working in both lps, join white in 2nd sc of any 3-sc group; ch 1, 3 sc in same sc: corner made*; ** sc in next 5 sc; sk next 9 sc, sc in next 2 sc, ch 4; working behind next point, skip next 7 sc, sc in next 2 sc, sk next 9 sc, sc in next 5 sc **; 3 sc in next sc: corner made; rep from * twice more, then rep from ** to ** once; join in first sc: square formed; finish off white.

Rnd 9: With larger hook join blue with sl st, in any corner, ch 1, *3 sc in same st; sc in next 7 sts, skip next st, 4 sc in ch-4 sp, skip next st, sc in next 7 sts, 3 sc in next st for corner; rep from * 3 times more, ending last rep with sc in last 7 sts; join; finish off blue.

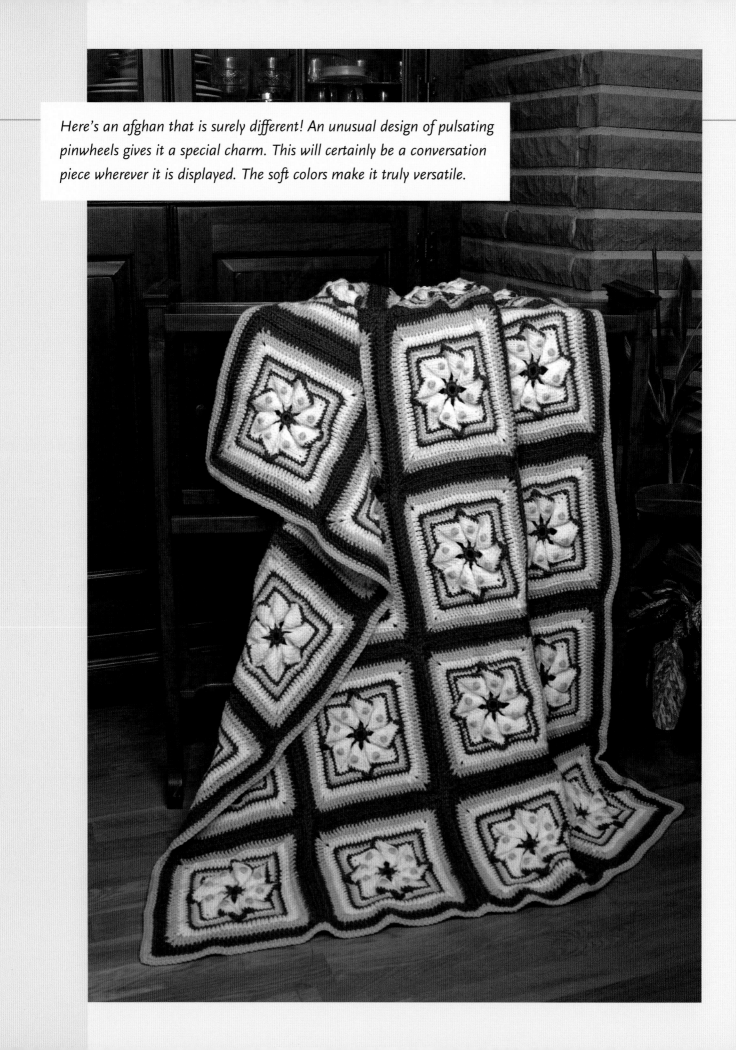

Here's an afghan that is surely different! An unusual design of pulsating pinwheels gives it a special charm. This will certainly be a conversation piece wherever it is displayed. The soft colors make it truly versatile.

Rnd 10: With smaller hook, join mauve in center sc of any 3-sc corner group, 3 sc in same st; sc in each st around, working 3 sc in center st of reach rem corner; join, finish off mauve.

Rnd 11: Join white in center sc of any corner, (ch 3, dc, ch 2, 2 dc) in same st; dc in each st around, working (2 dc, ch 2, 2 dc) in each corner st; finish off white.

Rnd 12: With blue, rep Rnd 11; finish off blue.

Rnd 13: With mauve, rep Rnd 11; finish off mauve, weave in all ends.

Joining

To join squares, hold 2 squares with right sides tog and sew along one edge with mauve, carefully matching sts and corners. Join in 5 rows of 4 squares each.

Edging

Hold piece with right side facing; join blue in outer corner st at upper right.

Rnd 1: Ch 1, 3 sc in same st; sc in each st around, working 3 sc in each outer corner sp and adjusting sts to keep work flat; join.

Rnd 2: Sl st into next sc, ch 1, 3 sc in same st; sc in each st around, working 3 sc in each outer corner st; join, finish off, weave in ends.

The classic beauty of the traditional knitted Fisherman Afghan with its intricate designs is translated here into a work for crocheters. The knitters of the Aran Isles gave us a gift that has been handed down for generations, and now crocheters can use it too.

crochet
Aran Afghan

Designed by Margret Willson

SIZE
48" x 63"

MATERIALS
Worsted weight yarn,
  60 oz off white
*Note: Photographed model made with TLC® Essentials™
  #2313 Aran*
Size I (5.5 mm) crochet hook (or size required
  for gauge)

GAUGE
12dc = 4"

STITCH GUIDE

Front post triple crochet (Fptr): YO twice, insert
hook from front to back to front around post (vertical
bar) of specified st, (YO and draw through 2 lps) 3
times: Fptr made.

Front post double triple (FPdtr): YO 3 times, insert
hook from front to back to front around post (vertical
bar) of specified st, (YO and draw through 2 lps) 4
times: Fpdtr made.

*Note: All post sts are worked around next or specified st 2
rows below; for each post st, skip one sc on working row.*

Cluster (Cl): Keeping last lp of each st on hook, work
5 dc in specified st, YO and draw through all 6 lps on
hook: Cl made.

Puff st (Pst): (YO, insert hook in specified st, YO and
draw lp through) 4 times, YO and draw through 8 lps,
YO and draw through last 2 lps: Pst made.

Instructions
Ch 160.

Row 1 (right side): Dc in 4th ch from hook (do not
count beg ch-3 as a st) dc in each of next 13 chs; *[ch 1,
skip next ch, dc in next ch, ch 1, skip next ch; dc in
each of next 23 chs; ch 1, skip next ch, dc in next ch,
ch 1, skip next ch]; dc in each of next 21 chs; rep from

* once more, rep between [ ] once, ending dc in last 14
chs, turn.

Row 2: Ch 1, sc in next 14 sts; *[sc in next ch-1 sp, Cl
in next dc, sc in next sp, sc in next 11 sts, Pst in next dc
(center st of diamond); sc in next 11 sc, sc in next ch-1
sp, Cl in next dc, sc in next ch-1 sp], sc in next 21 sts;
rep from * once more, rep between [ ] once, ending sc
in last 14 sts, turn.

Note: Remember to work post sts two rows below.

Row 3: Ch 3 (counts as first dc), skipping beg ch-3 and
first dc of Row 1, work (Fptr, dc) 4 times, Fptr, *[3 dc,
Fptr, ch 1, skip next sc, dc in Cl, ch 1, skip next sc,
(Fptr, 3 dc) skip next st 2 rows below, Fpdtr around
each of the 2 sts before center st of diamond; skip next
2 sc on working row, dc in next sc, dc in Pst, dc in next
sc; Fpdtr around the 2 sts following center st, skip 2 sc
on working row (3 dc, Fptr) twice; ch 1, skip next sc,
dc in Cl, ch 1, skip next sc, Fptr, 3 dc]; (Fptr, dc) 6
times, Fptr; rep from * once more, rep between [ ]
once; (Fptr, dc) 5 times, turn.

Row 4: Ch 1, 14 sc; *[sc in next sp, Cl in next dc, sc in
next sp, 10 sc; Pst, sc, Pst, 10 sc, sc in next sp, Cl in
next dc, sc in next sp], 21 sc; rep from * once more, rep
between [ ] once, ending 14 sc, turn.

Row 5: Ch 3, (dc, Fptr) 4 times, 4 dc; *[Fptr, ch 1, skip
sc, dc in Cl, ch 1, skip sc Fptr, 3 dc, Fptr, 2 dc; Fpdtr
around each of next 2 Fptr, (dc in next sc, dc in next
Pst) twice, dc in next sc, Fpdtr around each of next 2
Fptr; 2 dc, Fptr, 3 dc, Fptr, ch 1, skip sc, dc in Cl, ch 1,
skip sc, Fptr, 4 dc]; (Fptr, dc) 6 times, 3 dc; rep from *
once more, rep between [ ] once, ending (Fptr, dc) 4
times, dc, turn.

Row 6: Ch 1, 14 sc; *[sc in next sp, Cl in next dc, sc in
next sp, 9 sc; (Pst, sc) twice, Pst, 9 sc, sc in next sp; Cl
in next dc, sc in next sp]; 21 sc, rep from * once more,
rep between [ ] once, ending 14 sc, turn.

Row 7: Ch 3, (Fptr, dc) 4 times, Fptr, 3 dc; *[Fptr, ch 1,
dc in Cl, ch 1, Fptr, 3 dc, Fptr, dc, Fpdtr around each of

next 2 Fpdtr; (dc in next sc, dc in next Pst) 3 times, dc in next sc; Fpdtr around each of next 2 Fpdtr, dc, Fptr, 3 dc, Fptr; ch 1, dc in Cl, ch 1, Fptr, 3 dc]; (Fptr, dc) 6 times, Fptr, 3 dc; rep from * once more, rep between [ ] once, ending (Fptr, dc) 5 times, turn.

Row 8: Ch 1, 14 sc; *[sc in sp, Cl in dc, sc in sp, 8 sc; (Pst, sc) 3 times, Pst, 8 sc, sc in sp, Cl in dc, sc in sp], 21 sc; rep from * once more, rep between [ ] once, ending 14 sc, turn.

Row 9: Ch 3, (dc, Fptr) 4 times, 4 dc; *[Fptr, ch 1, dc in Cl, ch 1, Fptr, 3 dc, Fptr, 2 dc; Fpdtr around each of next 2 Fpdtr, sk next Pst, (dc in sc, dc in Pst) twice, dc in sc; Fpdtr around each of next 2 Fpdtr, 2 dc, Fptr, 3 dc, Fptr, ch 1, dc in Cl, ch 1, Fptr, 4 dc]; (Fptr, dc) 6 times, 3 dc; rep from * once more, rep between [ ] once, ending (Fptr, dc) 4 times, dc, turn.

Row 10: Rep Row 6.

Row 11: Ch 3, (Fptr, dc) 4 times, Fptr, 3 dc; *[Fptr, ch 1, dc in Cl, ch 1, (Fptr, 3 dc) twice; Fpdtr around each of next 2 Fpdtr, sk next Pst, dc in next sc, dc in Pst, dc in next sc; sk next Pst, Fpdtr around each of next 2 Fpdtr, 3 dc, Fptr, 3 dc, Fptr; ch 1, dc in Cl, ch 1, Fptr, 3 dc]; (Fptr, dc) 6 times, Fptr, 3 dc; rep from * once more, rep between [ ] once, ending (Fptr, dc) 5 times, turn.

Row 12: Rep Row 4.

Row 13: Ch 3, (dc, Fptr) 4 times, 4 dc; *[Fptr, ch 1, dc in Cl, ch 1, Fptr, 3 dc, Fptr, 4 dc; Fpdtr around each of next 2 Fpdtr, sk next Pst, dc in next sc, sk next Pst, Fpdtr around each of next 2 Fpdtr; 4 dc, Fptr, 3 dc, Fptr, ch 1, dc in next Cl, ch 1, Fptr, 4 dc]; (Fptr, dc) 6 times, 3 dc; rep from * once more, rep between [ ] once, ending (Fptr, dc) 4 times, dc, turn.

Row 14: Rep Row 2.

Row 15: Ch 3, (Fptr, dc) 4 times, Fptr, 3 dc; *[Fptr, ch 1, dc in Cl, ch 1, Fptr, 3 dc, Fptr, 5 dc; Fpdtr around next Fpdtr, keeping last lp of each on hook, Fpdtr around next Fpdtr, dc in Pst, Fpdtr around next Fpdtr, YO and draw through all 4 lps on hook; Fpdtr around next Fpdtr, 5 dc, Fptr, 3 dc, Fptr, ch 1, dc in Cl; ch 1, Fptr, 3 dc]; (Fptr, dc) 6 times, 3 dc; rep from * once more, rep between [ ] once, ending (Fptr, dc) 5 times, turn.

Row 16: Ch 1, 14 sc; *[sc in next sp, Cl in next dc, sc in next sp; 23 sc, sc in next sp, Cl in next dc, sc in next sp], 21 sc; rep from * once more, rep between [ ] once, ending 14 sc, turn.

Row 17: Ch 3, (dc, Fptr) 4 times, 4 dc; *[Fptr, ch 1, dc in CL, ch 1, Fptr, 3 dc, Fptr, 4 dc, skip 2 Fpdtr; Fpdtr around each of next 2 Fpdtr, skip next 2 sc, dc in next sc, Fpdtr around each of 2 skipped Fpdtr; sk next 2 sc, 4 dc, Fptr, 3 dc, Fptr, ch 1, dc in Cl, ch 1, Fptr, 4 dc]; (Fptr, dc) 6 times, 3 dc; rep from * once more, rep between [ ] once, (Fptr, dc) 4 times, dc in last st, turn.

Row 18: Rep Row 2.

Row 19: Ch 3, (Fptr, dc) 4 times, Fptr; *[3 dc, Fptr, ch 1, dc in Cl, ch 1, (Fptr, 3 dc) twice, Fpdtr around each of next 2 Fpdtr, sk 2 sc; dc in next sc, dc in Pst, dc in next sc, Fpdtr around each of next 2 Fpdtr, sk 2 sc; dc in each of next 3 sc, Fptr, 3 dc, Fptr, ch 1, dc in Cl, ch 1, Fptr, 3 dc]; (Fptr, dc) 6 times, Fptr; rep from * once more, rep between [ ] once, ending (Fptr, dc) 5 times, turn.

Rep Rows 4 through 19 nine more times, then rep Rows 2 through 14 once.

Last Row: Ch 3, (Fptr, dc) 4 times, Fptr; *[3 dc, Fptr, ch 1, dc in Cl, ch 1, Fptr, 3 dc, Fptr, 4 dc; Fpdtr around each of next 2 Fpdtr, dc in Ps, Fpdtr around each of next 2 Fpdtr, 4 dc; Fptr, 3 dc, Fptr, ch 1, dc in Cl , ch 1, Fptr, 3 dc]; (Fptr, dc) 6 times, Fptr; rep from * once more, rep between [ ] once, ending (Fptr, dc) 5 times, finish off.

Edging

With right side facing, join yarn with sc in lower right-hand corner, 2 sc in same corner; [working up side edge, *sc around end of dc row, sc around edge of next sc row, 2 sc around end of next dc row, sc around next sc row, rep from * to corner, 3 sc in corner, ch 1, sk next st; **sc in each of next 2 sts or sps, ch 1, sk next st or sp, rep from ** across to corner]; 3 sc in corner, rep between [ ], join with sl st in beg sc; finish off. Weave in all ends.

Fringe

Following Triple Knot Fringe instructions on page 127, cut yarn strands 24" long. Knot 4 strands in each ch-1 sp across top and bottom (8 strands each fringe after folding), finish as for Triple Knot Fringe. Trim fringe.

crochet

Raspberries and Cream

designed by Janie Herrin

SIZE
48" x 60" before border

MATERIALS
Worsted weight yarn,
  30 oz raspberry
  24 oz white
Note: *Photographed model made with Caron® Simply Soft® #2678 Raspberry and #2602 White*
Size H (5mm) crochet hook (or size required for gauge)

GAUGE
7 dc = 2"
Square = 12" x 12"

STITCH GUIDE

Front Post Single Crochet (FPsc): Insert hook from front to back to front around post (vertical bar) of specified st, YO and draw lp through, YO and draw through both lps on hook: FPsc made.

Instructions

Square (make 20)
With raspberry, ch 5, join with a sl st to form a ring.

Rnd 1: Ch 3, in ring work 2 dc, ch 2, (3 dc, ch 2) 3 times; join with sl st in beg ch-3: 4 ch-2 sps.

Rnd 2: Ch 3, dc in next 2 sts, in next sp work (2 dc, ch 2, 2 dc): corner made; (dc in next 3 sts, work corner) 3 times; join with sl st in beg ch-3.

Rnd 3: Ch 3, dc in next 4 sts, work corner, (dc in next 7 sts, work corner) 3 times, dc in next 2 dc; join with sl st in beg ch-3.

Rnd 4: Ch 3, dc in next 6 sts, work corner, (dc in next 11 sts, work corner) 3 times, dc in next 4 dc; join with sl st in 3rd ch of beg ch-3; finish off raspberry.

Rnd 5: Join white with sc in any ch-2 corner sp, ch 2, sc in same sp; *sc in next 2 sts, ch 5, FPsc around post of first dc below on Rnd 2, (ch 5, skip 2 sts, sc in next st on Rnd 4, ch 5, skip next dc on Rnd 2, FPsc around next dc) 3 times, ch 5, skip 2 sts, sc in next 2 sts on Rnd 4, in corner sp work (sc, ch 2, sc); rep from * 3 times more, ending with sc in last 2 sts on Rnd 4, sl st in beg sc.

Rnd 6: Ch 3; * in next corner sp work (2 dc, ch 2, 2 dc); dc in next 3 sc, (dc in each of next 2 dc of Rnd 4, dc in sc of Rnd 5) 4 times, dc in next 2 sc; rep from * 3 times more ending with dc in last sc; join in beg ch-3.

Rnd 7: Ch 3, dc in each st to ch-2 sp, work corner in sp, (dc in each st across to next sp, work corner) 3 times, dc in rem dc; sl st in beg ch-3.

Rnd 8: Rep Rnd 7; at end finish off white.

Rnd 9: Join raspberry with sc in any corner sp, ch 2, sc in same sp; *sc in next 3 sts, ch 5, FPsc around post of first dc below on Rnd 6, (ch 5, skip 3 sts, sc in next st on Rnd 9, ch 5, skip next 3 dc on Rnd 6, FPsc around post of next dc) 5 times, ch 5, skip 3 sts, sc in next 3 sts on Rnd 9, in corner sp work (sc, ch 2, sc); rep from * 3 times more, ending with sc in last 3 sc, sl st in beg sc.

Rnd 10: Ch 3; *(dc, ch 2, dc) in corner sp, (dc in next 3 sts, ch 1, skip next st) 7 times, dc in next 3 sts; rep from * around, ending with sl sst in beg ch-3; finish off raspberry.

Rnd 11: Join white with sc in any corner sp, ch 2, sc in same sp; *sc in next 4 dc; working in front of ch-1 sp, (tr in skipped sc 2 rounds below, sc in next 3 dc) 7 times, sc in next dc, (sc, ch 2, sc) in corner sp; rep from * around, ending with sl st in beg sc; finish off.

Rnd 12: Join raspberry in any ch-2 corner sp, ch 3, 2 dc in same sp; dc in each st around working 3 dc in each rem corner sp, end with sl st in beg ch-3; finish off; weave in ends.

It's so "delicious" that our kitty couldn't resist resting comfortably on this vibrant, combination of colors which helps create a fine example of the crocheter's art You'll enjoy working these large squares in an interesting technique.

Joining

To join, hold two squares with right sides tog and with raspberry sew tog with overcast st along one side edge, carefully matching sts and corners. Then in same manner join into 5 rows of 4 squares each.

Border

Rnd 1: Hold afghan with right side facing you; join raspberry with sc in outer corner sp at top right; ch 1, 3 sc in same sp; sc around entire out edge of afghan, working 3 sc in each outer corner sp; join.

Rnd 2: Sl st in next sc, ch 3, 2 dc in same sc; *dc in each sc to next corner, 3 dc in center sc of each 3-sc corner sp; rep from * around; join in 3rd ch of beg ch-3. Finish off raspberry.

Rnd 3: Join white with sc in any dc; *sc in next dc; rep from * around, join in beg dc; finish off; weave in all yarn ends.

What a wonderful gift for the new baby for its Christening, dedication or naming ceremony! With its wide lacey ruffle, this spectacular piece is sure to become a family heirloom and to be used for generations of new babies.

crochet
A Special Welcome

Designed by Nazanin S. Fard

SIZE
40" square before border

MATERIALS
Baby weight yarn,
  24 oz white
Note: Photographed model made with Plymouth Dreambaby #100 White
Size F (3.75 mm) crochet hook (or size required for gauge)

GAUGE
24 sc = 4"

STITCH GUIDE

dc2tog decrease (dc2tog): (YO, insert hook in next st and draw up a lp, YO and draw through first 2 lps) twice, YO and draw through all 3 lps on hook: dc2tog made.

Puff Stitch (Pst): YO, insert hook in next st, YO and draw up a lp; (YO, insert hook in same st, YO and draw up a lp) twice; YO and draw through all 7 lps on hook: Pst made.

Shell: (sc, ch 4, sc) in same st.

Shell in Shell: (sc, ch 4, sc) in ch-4 sp of next shell.

PATTERN STITCH

Row 1: Dc in 4th ch from hook, (dc2tog) 2 times; * (ch 1, Pst in next ch) 5 times, ch 1, (dc2tog) 6 times; rep from * across to last 6 sts, (dc2tog) 3 times; ch 1, turn.

Row 2: Sc in each st and ch-1 sp; ch 3, turn.

Row 3: Sk first sc, dc in next st, (dc2tog) 2 times; * (ch 1, Pst in next st) 5 times, ch 1, (dc2tog) 6 times; rep from * across to last 6 sts, ch 1, (dc2tog) 3 times; ch 1, turn.

Rep Rows 2 and 3 for pattern.

Instructions
Ch 223.

Follow Pattern Stitch until piece measures about 40", ending by working a Row 2; at end of last rnd, ch 1, turn; do not cut yarn.

Edging

Rnd 1: 3 sc in first sc for corner; sc in each sc across to last sc, 3 sc in last sc for corner; sc along side, working sc in side of sc rows and 2 sc in dc rows, adjusting sts to keep work flat; 3 sc in last row for corner; continue working around in same manner, working 3 sc in last st of last row for corner, and up last side as before; join with sl st in beg sc.

Border

Rnd 1: In next sc work (sc, ch 4, sc): shell made; * ch 3, sk 3 sc, shell in next sc; rep from * around, join with sl st in beg sc (***Note:*** *You may need to sk 2 sc instead of 3 a few times to come out even on this rnd only).*

Rnds 2 through 7: Sl st in ch-4 sp of next shell, shell in same sp; *ch 4, shell in next shell; rep from * around, join with sl st in beg sc.

Rnds 8 through 12: Sl st in ch-4 sp of next shell, shell in same sp; * ch 5, shell in next shell; rep from * around, join with sl st in beg sc.

Rnds 13 through 21: Sl st in ch-4 sp of next shell, shell in same sp; *ch 6, shell in next shell; rep from * around, join as before.

Rnd 22: Sl st in ch-4 sp of next shell, shell in same sp; *ch 7, shell in next shell; rep from * around, join.

Rnd 23: *In next shell work (2 sc, ch 3, 2 sc); in next ch-7 sp work (4 sc, ch 3, 4 sc); rep from * around, join with sl st in beg sc; finish off, weave in ends.

Soft as a whisper and light as a breeze, this wonderful afghan is made in the thinnest mohair and silk-blend yarn in an open stitch that shows off the beauty of the yarn. The throw offers just enough warmth for a chilly summer evening, or an afternoon nap.

crochet
Stitches in Time

Designed by Ruthie Marks

SIZE
47" x 47"

MATERIALS
Lace weight mohair/silk blend yarn,
   10½ oz rose
*Note: Photographed model made with Knit One,
   Crochet Too Douceur et Soie # 8248 Velvet Rose*
Size G (4.5 mm) crochet hook (or size required
   for gauge)
6" of contrasting yarn for marker
Stitch marker

GAUGE
(Sc, ch 3, sc) = ¾"
1 rnd = ¾"

NOTES
1. Because the yarn is so fine, it helps to see where to put the hook in Rnd 2 if you insert a contrasting color yarn marker before closing the ch in Rnd 1. Remove marker after Rnd 2.

2. Place st marker in ending sc of each round, and move it up as you work.

Instructions

Rnd 1: Starting at center of throw, ch 4, insert yarn marker, join with a sl st in beg ch.

Rnd 2: (Sc, ch 3, sc: corner made;) in each ch, sl st in back lp of first sc: 4 corners made.

Rnd 3: Sl st in top lp of first ch of Rnd 2, (sc, ch 3, sc, ch 3) in each corner ch-3 sp, sl st in back lp of first sc.

Rnd 4: Sl st in top lp of first ch of last rnd, (sc, ch 3, sc, ch 3) in first corner ch-3 sp, (sc, ch 3) in first ch-3 sp following corner; *(sc, ch 3, sc, ch 3) in next corner ch-3 sp, (sc, ch 3) in next ch-3 sp following corner; rep from * around, sl st in back lp of first sc: one (sc, ch 3) between corners on each side.

Rep Rnd 4, increasing one (sc, ch 3) between corners on each side on each rnd, until there are 61 ch-3 sps between corners (or work to desired size). Sl st in back lp of first sc, finish off, weave in ends.

Fringe

Winding yarn loosely around a 6" piece of cardboard, cut 392 strands. Gather 10 strands for the ch-3 space in each corner, and 4 strands for each of the 11 ch-3 spaces on each side of each corner. Knot fringes in the ch-3 spaces, trim fringe.

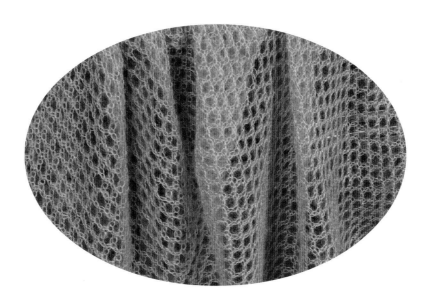

Do you have a friend who loves the country decorating style? Then this throw is the perfect gift for her! An unusual technique is used in the crisp points at either end to create a striking edging. The gingham pattern is a long-time favorite.

knit
Glorious Gingham

Designed by Jodi Lewanda

SIZE
45" x 55"

MATERIALS
Worsted weight yarn,
  30 oz lt grey (A)
  18 oz dk grey (B)
  5 oz white (C)
*Note: Photographed model made with Lion Brand®
  Wool-Ease®*
#151 Grey Heather (A); #152 Oxford Grey (B) and
  #100 White (C)
Size 10½ (6.5 mm) knitting needles (or size required
  for gauge)

GAUGE
15 sts = 4" with 2 strands of yarn held tog,
24 rows = 4"

Instructions

Note: Work with 2 strands of yarn held tog throughout.

Strip 1 (make 7):

Beginning at point edge with 2 strands of A, CO 2 sts.

Row 1: Knit.

Row 2: Inc (knit in front and back of st) in first st, knit rem sts: 3 sts

Row 3 through 12: Rep Row 2: 13 sts at end of Row 12.

Square 1
Change to B.

Rows 1 through 22: Knit.

Square 2
Change to A.

Rows 1 through 20: *K1, P1; rep from * across row to last st, ending K 1.

Rep Squares 1 and 2, 6 more times; rep Square 1, once: 15 squares made.

Ending Point Edge
Row 1: Knit.

Row 2: Knit to last 2 stitches, K2tog.

Rep Row 2 until 2 sts remain. BO; weave in ends.

Strip 2 (make 6)
Beginning at point edge with 2 strands of C, CO 2 sts.

Row 1: Knit.

Row 2: Inc (knit in front and back of same st), knit across: 3 sts.

Rows 3 through 12: Rep Row 2: 13 sts at end of Row 12.

Square 1
Change to B.

Row 1 (right side): Knit.

Row 2: *K1, P1, rep from * across, ending K 1.

Rows 3 through 20: Rep Row 2.

Square 2
Change to C.

Row 1 (right side): Knit.

Rows 2 through 4: Purl.

Row 5: Knit.

Row 6: Purl.

Rows 7 through 9: Knit.

Row 10: Purl.

Row 11: Knit.

Rows 12 through 14: Purl.

Row 15: Knit.

Row 16: Purl.

Rows 17 through 19: Knit.

Row 20: Purl.

Rep Squares 1 and 2, 6 more times, then rep Square 1, once: 15 squares made.

Ending point edge
Change to C.

Row 1: Knit.

Row 2: Knit to last 2 sts, K2tog.

Rep Row 2 until 2 sts rem. BO, weave in ends.

Joining

Being sure all right sides face the same way, sew strips together starting with Strip 1, then Strip 2; alternate Strips 1 and 2 across, ending with Strip 1; leave points loose at each end.

Weave in all ends

knit
Harlequin Panels

Designed by Patons Design Staff

SIZE
47" x 54½"

MATERIALS
Worsted weight yarn
  21 oz burgundy(MC)
  21 oz taupe(A)
*Note: Photographed model made with Patons® Décor
  #1647 Burgundy and #1631 Taupe*
Size 7 (4.5 mm) knitting needles (or size required
  for gauge)
36" Size 5 (3.75 mm) circular knitting needle
6" wide cardboard

GAUGE
20 sts = 4" with larger needles in stockinette st (knit
  one row, purl one row)
26 rows = 4"

STITCH GUIDE

Inc 1 = knit into front and back of next st

Inc 1P = purl into front and back of next st

Instructions

*Note: To change colors, twist the two colors around each
other where they meet, on wrong side, to avoid a hole.*

Strip (make 7)

With MC and larger needles cast on 19 sts, with A cast
on 19 sts: 38sts.

Row 1 (wrong side): With A, K19. With MC, K19.

Row 2: With MC, Kl, inc 1, K15, K2tog. With A, sl 1,
K1, PSSO, knit to last 3 sts, inc 1, K2.

Row 3: Rep Row 1.

Row 4: With MC, Kl, (YO, K2tog) 9 times. With A, sl
1, Kl, PSSO, (YO, K2tog) 8 times, YO, K1.

Rows 5, 7, 9 and 11: With A, P19. With MC, P19.

Rows 6, 8, 10 and 12: With MC, P1, inc 1P, P15,
P2tog. With A, P2tog, purl to last 3 sts, inc 1P, P2.

Row 13: With A, (P2tog,YRN) 9 times, Pl. With MC,
(P2tog, YRN) 9 times, Pl.

Rows 14, 16, 18, 20 and 22: Rep Row 2.

Row 15: With A, K19. With MC, K19.

Rows 17, 19, 21 and 23: With A, P19. With MC,
P19.

Row 24: With A, Kl, inc 1, K15, K2tog. With MC, sl 1,
K1, PSSO, knit to last 3 sts, inc l, K2.

Rows 25 and 27: With MC, K19. With A, K19.

Row 26: With A, K1, inc 1, K15, K2tog. With MC,
sl 1, Kl, PSSO, knit to last 3 sts, inc l, K2.

Row 28: With A, Kl, (YO, K2tog) 9 times. With MC,
sl 1, K1, PSSO, (YO, K2tog) 8 times, YO, K1.

Rows 29, 31, 33 and 35: With MC, P19. With A,
P19.

Rows 30, 32, 34 and 36: With A, Pl, inc lP, P15,
P2tog. With MC, P2tog, purl to last 3 sts, inc lP, P2.

Row 37: With MC, (P2tog, YRN) 9 times, Pl. With A,
(P2tog, YRN) 9 times, Pl.

Rows 38, 40, 42, 44 and 46: With A, K1, inc 1, K15,
K2tog. With MC, sl 1, Kl, PSSO, knit to last 3 sts, inc l,
K2.

Row 39: With MC, K19. With A, K19.

Rows 41, 43, 45 and 47: With MC, P19. With A,
P19.

Row 48: With MC, K1, inc 1, K15, K2tog. With A,
sl 1, Kl, PSSO, knit to last 3 sts, inc 1, K2.

Rep these 48 rows 7 times more. Then work Rows 1
through 3 once more. BO.

Just as the harlequin-patterned jester delighted his royal audience, so too will your very own royal person be delighted by the rich coloration and jaunty tassels of this delightful afghan, which is easy to knit in panels.

Finishing

Sew strips tog.

Side edging

With MC and smaller needles and right side of work facing pick up and knit 276 sts along one side edge.

Note: *Do not join; work back and forth in rows.*

Work 3 rows in garter st (knit every row). BO. Repeat along oppposite side edge.

Tassels (make 14)

Cut a piece of cardboard 6 " wide. Wind MC around cardboard 15 times. Cut yarn; then wind A around cardboard 15 times. Cut yarn leaving a long end. Thread end through a needle, and slip needle through all lps of MC and A and tie tightly. Remove cardboard and wind yarn tightly around loops 3/4" below fold. Fasten securely. Cut through rem loops and trim ends evenly. Sew tassels to points along cast-on and bound-off edges as shown in the photo.

A real tour de force for the knitter and a fabulous gift for a special friend, this afghan is one to be treasured forever. Here the ancient fabled stitches of the Aran Islands are interpreted once again in a dramatic and unique manner.

knit
Aran Textures

SIZE
55" x 60".

MATERIALS
Worsted weight yarn,
  54 oz off white
*Note: Photographed model made with Red Heart®
  Super Saver® # 313 Aran*
29" Size 9 (5.5 mm) circular knitting needle (or size
  required for gauge)
Cable needle

GAUGE
Strip 2 = 6½" wide
Strip 3 = 13½" wide

STITCH GUIDE

C2B = Sl next st onto cable needle and leave at back of
work, K1, then K1 from cable needle.

C2F = Sl next st onto cable needle and leave at front of
work, K1, then K1 from cable needle.

C6B = Sl next 3 sts onto cable needle and leave at back
of work, K3, then K3 from cable needle.

C5F = Sl next 3 sts onto cable needle and leave at front
of work, K2, sl the purl st from cable needle back onto
the left needle, P1, then K2 from cable needle.

KB1 = Knit into the back of the next st.

MB = (K1, KB1, K1, KB1, K1) all in next st: bobble
made

T2B = Sl next st onto cable needle and leave at back of
work, K1, then P1 from cable needle.

T2F = Sl next st onto cable needle and leave at front of
work, P1, then K1 from cable needle.

T3B = Sl next st onto cable needle and leave at back of
work, K2, then P1 from cable needle.

T3F = Slip next 2 sts onto cable needle and leave at
front of work, P1, then K2 from cable needle.

PATTERNS

Pattern A (worked over 10 sts)

Row 1 (wrong side): K2, P6, K2.

Row 2: P2, K6, P2.

Row 3: K2, P6, K2.

Row 4: P2, C6B, P2.

Rows 5 and 7: K2, P6, K2.

Row 6: P2, K6, P2.

Row 8: Rep Row 6.

Rows 1 through 8 form Pattern A.

Pattern B (worked over 19 sts)

Row 1 (wrong side): P1, K3, MB, K2, P2, K1, P2, K2, MB, K3, P1: 27 sts.

Row 2: K1, P3, K5tog tbl, P2, C5F, P2, K5 tog tbl, P3, K1: 19 sts.

Row 3: P1, K6, P2, K1, P2, K6, P1.

Row 4: K1, P5, T3B, P1, T3F, P5, K1.

Row 5: P1, K5, P2, K3, P2, K5, P1.

Row 6: K1, P4, T3B, P3, T3F, P4, K1.

Row 7: P1, K4, P2, K2, MB, K2, P2, K4, P1: 23 sts.

Row 8: K1, P3, T3B, P2, K5tog tbl, P2, T3F, P3, K1: 19 sts.

Row 9: P1, K3, P2, K7, P2, K3, P1.

Row 10: K1, P2, T3B, P7, T3F, P2, K1.

Row 11: P1, K2, P2, K2, MB, K3, MB, K2, P2, K2, P1: 27 sts.

Row 12: K1, P1, T3B, P2, K5tog tbl, P3, K5tog tbl, P2, T3F, P1, K1: 19 sts.

Row 13: P1, K1, P2, K11, P2, K1, P1.

Row 14: K1, P1, K2, P11, K2, P1, K1.

Row 15: P1, K1, P2, K3, MB, K3, MB, K3, P2, K1, P1: 27 sts.

Row 16: K1, P1, T3F, P2, K5tog tbl, P3, K5tog tbl, P2, T3B, P1, K1: 19 sts.

Row 17: P1, K2, P2, K9, P2, K2, P1.

Row 18: K1, P2, T3F, P7, T3B, P2, K1.

Row 19: P1, K3, P2, K3, MB, K3, P2, K3, P1: 23 sts.

Row 20: K1, P3, T3F, P2, K5tog tbl, P2, T3B, P3, K1: 19 sts.

Row 21: P1, K4, P2, K5, P2, K4, P1.

Row 22: K1, P4, T3F, P3, T3B, P4, K1.

Row 23: P1, K5, P2, K3, P2, K5, P1.

Row 24: K1, P5, T3F, P1, T3B, P5, K1.

Rows 1 through 24 form Pattern B.

Pattern C (worked over 16 sts)

Row 1 (wrong side): (K3, P2, K3) twice.

Row 2: (P3, C2B, P3) twice.

Row 3: Rep Row 1.

Row 4: (P2, T2B, T2F, P2) twice.

Row 5: (K2, P1) twice; K4, (P1, K2) twice.

Row 6: P1, T2B, P2, T2F, P2, T2B, P2, T2F, P1.

Row 7: K1, P1, K4, P1, K2, P1, K4, P1, K1.

Row 8: (T2B, P4, T2F) twice.

Row 9: P1, K6, P2, K6, P1.

Row 10: K1, P6, C2F, P6, K1.

Row 11: Rep Row 9.

Row 12: (T2F, P4, T2B) twice.

Row 13: Rep Row 7.

Row 14: P1, T2F, P2, T2B, P2, T2F, P2, T2B, P1.

Row 15: Rep Row 5.

Row 16: (P2, T2F, T2B, P2) twice.

Rows 1 through 16 form Pattern C.

Instructions

Strip 1 (make 1)

CO 78 sts.

Row 1 (wrong side): K4, work Patt B Row 1; work Patt A Row 1; work Patt C Row 1; work Patt A Row 1; work Patt B Row 1.

Row 2: Work Patt B Row 2; work Patt A Row 2; work Patt C Row 2; work Patt A Row 2; work Patt B Row 2; K4.

Row 3: K4; work Patt B Row 3; work Patt A Row 3; work Patt C Row 3; work Patt A Row 3; work Patt B Row 3.

Row 4: Work Patt B Row 4; work Patt A Row 4; work Patt C Row 4; work Patt A Row 4; work Patt B Row 4; K4.

Continue working appropriate rows of patterns until piece measures about 60" from CO row, ending by working Row 3 of Patt C. BO.

Strip 2 (make 2)

Cast on 38 sts.

Row 1 (wrong side): P1; work Patt A Row 1; work Patt C Row 1; work Patt A Row 1; P1.

Row 2: K1; work Patt A Row 2; work Patt C Row 2; work Patt A Row 2; K1.

Row 3: P1; work Patt A Row 3; work Patt C Row 3; work Patt A Row 3; P1.

Row 4: K1; work Patt A Row 4; work Patt C Row 4; work Patt A Row 4; K1.

Continue working appropriate rows of patterns until piece measures about 60" from CO row, ending by working Row 3 of Patt C. BO.

Strip 3 (make 1)

Cast on 74 sts.

Row 1 (wrong side): Work Patt B Row 1; work Patt A Row 1; work Patt C Row 1; work Patt A Row 1; work Patt B Row 1.

Row 2: Work Patt B Row 2;work Patt A Row 2; work Patt C Row 2; work Patt A Row 2; work Patt B Row 2.

Row 3: Work Patt B Row 3; work Patt A Row 3; work Patt C Row 3; work Patt A Row 3; work Patt B Row 3.

Row 4: Work Patt B Row 4; work Patt A Row 4; work Patt C Row 4; work Patt A Row 4; work Patt B Row 4.

Continue working appropriate rows of patterns until piece measures about 60" from beg, ending by working Row 3 of Patt C. BO.

Strip 4 (make 1)

Cast on 78 sts.

Row 1 (wrong side): Work Patt B Row 1; work Patt A Row 1; work Patt C Row 1; work Patt A Row 1; work Patt B Row 1; K4.

Row 2: K4; work Patt B Row 2; work Patt A Row 2; work Patt C Row 2; work Patt A Row 2; work Patt B Row 2.

Row 3: Work Patt B Row 3; work Patt A Row 3; work Patt C Row 3; work Patt A Row 3; work Patt B Row 3; K4.

Row 4: K4; work Patt Patt B Row 4; work Patt A Row 4; work Patt C Row 4; work Patt A Row 4; work Patt B Row 4.

Continue working appropriate rows of patterns until piece measures about 60" from beg, ending by working Row 3 of Patt C. BO

Finishing

Sew strips together following diagram.

Fringe

Following Fringe Instructions on page 127, cut 12" lengths of yarn. Holding 6 strands together, knot evenly along top and bottom edges of afghan.

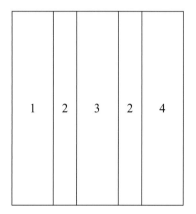

Every knitter loves a challenge, and this unusual creation provides it. The textured sections alternate with simple garter stitch, and the beautiful border adds the final touch. Make this afghan for someone you really love.

knit
A Knitter's Dream

Designed by Patons Design Staff

SIZE
41" x 49"

MATERIALS
Worsted-weight yarn,
  35 oz off white
*Note: Photographed model made with Patons® Décor
  #1602 Aran*
Size 7 (4.5 mm) knitting needles (or size required
  for gauge)

GAUGE
19 sts = 4" in garter st (knit each row)
38 garter st rows = 4 ins

STITCH GUIDE

Inc 1 = knit in front and back of next st

Instructions

*Note: Afghan can be worked in one piece or in separate
strips. To work afghan center as one piece, use a 36"
circular needle to cast on 160 sts, placing a marker after
every 32 sts to indicate the 5 sections worked as strips.
Work back and forth on circular needle across all stitches
on each row, working as for Strip A on first section, B on
the next section, followed by A, B, and A on the rem
sections. Work to length indicated for strips, BO all sts.
Work border and attach to edges of afghan center.*

Strip A (make 3)
Cast on 32 sts.

Row 1 (wrong side): Knit.

Rows 2 through 49: Knit.

Row 50: K3; *YO, K8, YO, Kl; rep from * to last 2 sts,
K2: 38 sts.

Row 51: K4; *P8, K3; rep from * to last st, K1.

Row 52: K4; *YO, K8, YO,K3; rep from * to last st,
K1: 44 sts.

Row 53: K5; *P8, K5; rep from * across.

Row 54: K5; *YO, K8, YO, K5; rep from * across:
50 sts.

Row 55: K6; *P8, K7; rep from * to last 14 sts; P8, K6.

Row 56: K6; *K4tog tbl, K4tog, K7; rep from * to last
14 sts; K4tog tbl, K4tog, K6: 32 sts.

Rows 57 through 96: Rep Rows 49 through 56 five
more times.

Rep Rows 1 through 96 twice more, then knit Rows 1
through 49 once more. BO.

Strip B (make 2)
CO 32 sts.

Row 1 (wrong side): Knit.

Row 2: K3; *YO, K8, YO, Kl; rep from * to last 2 sts,
K2: 38 sts.

Row 3: K4; *P8, K3; rep from * to last st, K1.

Row 4: K4; *YO, K8, YO, K3; rep from * to last st, K1:
44 sts.

Row 5: K5; *P8, K5; rep from * across.

Row 6: K5; *YO, K8, YO, K5; rep from * across: 50 sts.

Row 7: K6; *P8, K7; rep from * to last 14 sts; P8, K6.

Row 8: K6; *K4tog tbl, K4tog, K7; rep from * to last 14
sts; K4tog tbl, K4tog, K6: 32 sts.

Rows 9 through 48: Rep Rows 1 through 8 five more
times.

Rows 49 through 96: Knit.

Rep Rows 1 through 96 twice more, then knit Rows 1
through 49 once more. BO.

Finishing

Sew strips tog alternating strip A with strip B as shown
in photo, and carefully matching rows.

Border

CO 7 sts.

Row 1 (wrong side): Knit.

Row 2: K6, inc 1: 8 sts.

Row 3: Inc 1, K7: 9 sts.

Row 4: K8, inc 1: 10 sts.

Row 5: Inc 1, K9: 11 sts.

Row 6: K10, inc 1: 12 sts.

Row 7: Inc 1, K11: 13 sts.

Row 8: K12, inc 1: 14 sts.

Row 9: Inc 1, K13: 15 sts.

Row 10: K13, K2tog: 14 sts.

Row 11: K2tog, K12: 13 sts.

Row 12: K11, K2tog: 12 sts.

Row 13: K2tog, K10: 11 sts.

Row 14: K9, K2tog: 10 sts.

Row 15: K2tog, K8: 9 sts.

Row 16: K7, K2tog: 8 sts.

Row 17: K2tog, K6: 7 sts.

Rep last 17 rows until edging from CO edge measures sufficient length to fit around outer edge, allowing extra length for gathering at corners, ending with Row 17 of patt. BO. With rights sides tog, pin edging to afghan, gathering at corners. Sew border to afghan. Sew ends of border tog.

knit
Graphic Blocks

Designed by Patons Design Staff

SIZE
46½" x 52"

MATERIALS
Worsted weight yarn,
  7 oz medium grey (A)
  7 oz dark grey (B)
  7 oz gold (C)
  10½ oz periwinkle (D)
  7 oz green (E)
  7 oz variegated (F)
  10½ oz beige (G)
  7 oz orange (H)
Note: Photographed model made with Patons® Canadiana #311 Mediium Grey Heather (A), #312 Dark Grey Mix (B), #81 Gold (C), #140 Dark Periwinkle (D), #47 Jade (E), #438 Rainbow Variegated (F), #304 Beige (G) and #72 Orange (H)
Size 8 (5 mm) knitting needles (or size required for gauge)

GAUGE
18 sts= 4" in garter st (knit each row)
34 garter st rows = 4"

Note: When working with more than one color within a row, use separate balls or bobbins for each area of color. To change colors, twist the two colors around each other where they meet, on wrong side, to avoid a hole.

Instructions

Strip A (make 3)
With G, CO 35 sts.

Rows 1 through 8: With G, knit.

Row 9: With H, K5. With G, K30.

Row 10: With G, K30. With H, K5.

Rows 11 through 16: Rep Rows 9 and 10.

Row 17: With H, K10. With G, K25.

Row 18: With G, K25. With H, K10.

Rows 19 through 24: Rep Rows 17 and 18

Row 25: With H, K15. With G, K20.

Row 26: With G, K20. With H, K15.

Rows 27 through 32: Rep Rows 25 and 26.

Row 33: With H, K20. With G, K15.

Row 34: With G, K15. With H, K20.

Rows 35 through 40: Rep Rows 33 and 34.

Row 41: With H, K25. With G, K10.

Row 42: With G, K10. With H, K25.

Rows 43 through 48: Rep Rows 41 and 42.

Row 49: With H, K30. With G, K5.

Row 50: With G, K5. With H, K30.

Rows 51 through 56: Rep Rows 49 and 50.

Rows 57 through 64: With H, knit.

Rows 65 through 72: With E, knit.

Row 73: With F, K5. With E, K30.

Row 74: With E, K30. With F, K5.

Rows 75 through 80: Rep Rows 73 and 74.

Row 81: With F, K10. With E, K25.

Row 82: With E, K25. With F, K10.

Rows 83 through 88: Rep Rows 81 and 82.

Row 89: With F, K15. With E, K20.

Row 90: With E, K20. With F, K15

Rows 91 through 96: Rep Rows 89 and 90.

Row 97: With F, K20. With E, K15.

Row 98: With E, K15. With F, K20.

Rows 99 through 104: Rep Rows 97 and 98.

Row 105: With F, K25. With E, K10.

Color and motion are combined in this brilliantly graphic afghan straight from the painter's palette. You'll love watching it grow under your fingers as you "paint" with the many colors of yarn.

Row 106: With E, K10. With F, K25.

Rows 107 through 112: Rep Rows 105 and 106.

Row 113: With F, K30. With E, K5.

Row 114: With E, K5. With F, K30.

Rows 115 through 120: Rep Rows 113 and 114.

Rows 121 through 128: With F, knit.

Rep Rows 1 through 128 twice more, then rep Rows 1 through 64 once; BO as to knit. Weave in yarn ends.

Strip B (make 3)

Work as given for Strip A substituting C for G, D for H, A for E and B for F.

Finishing

Sew strips tog, alternating Strip A and Strip B, carefully matching rows and taking care not to stretch work.

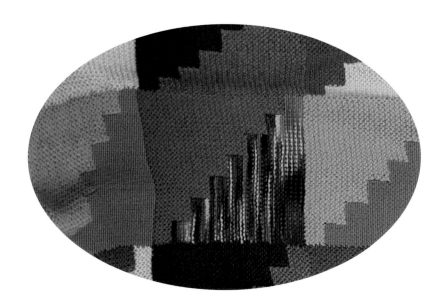

Once men sailed thousands of miles to obtain the fibers of rare cashmere and silk. Today we can use them to crochet a truly a luxurious afghan with quiet elegance. The pattern shows the fibers at their best, and is a pleasure to work.

crochet
Treasures from the East

Designed by Ruthie Marks

SIZE
31" x 45"

MATERIALS
Fingering weight yarn,
  8.7 oz (1,460 yds) red (A)
Lace weight eyelash yarn,
  5½ oz (1,140 yds) red (B)
Note: *Photographed model made with Knit One Crochet Too Richesse et Soie #9359 Pimento (A); and Sprinkles #243 Garnet (B)*
Size G (4 mm) crochet hook (or size required
  for gauge)
Size H (5 mm) crochet hook

GAUGE
2 rows = 1" with smaller hook and one strand of each
  yarn held tog

Instructions

With larger hook and one strand of each yarn held tog, ch 173; change to smaller hook.

Row 1: With smaller hook, sc in 2nd ch from hook, skip 2 chs, 3 dc in next ch; *ch 4, skip 4 chs, sc in next ch, skip 2 chs, 3 dc in next ch; rep from * across, turn.

Row 2: Ch 1, sc in first dc, 3 dc in next sc; *ch 4, sc in ch-4 space, 3 dc in next sc; rep from * across, turn.

Repeat Row 2 for pattern until piece measures 45" long. Finish off, weave in ends.

Fringe

Following Fringe Instructions on page 127, cut 12" strands of Color A and work Single Knot Fringe, using 8 strands in each knot and tying one knot in each ch-4 sp across each end of throw.

The colors of a dramatic sunset over a Western landscape are reflected in this wonderful afghan. The striking zig-zag pattern is reminiscent of design themes used by Native Americans on their revered pottery.

crochet
Zig-Zag

Designed by Linda Taylor

SIZE
50" x 64"

MATERIALS:
Worsted weight yarn,
  1,824 yds teal (A);
  2,052 yds gold (B)
  1,140 yds rust (C)
Size H (5 mm) afghan hook (or size required
  for gauge)
Size G (4 mm) crochet hook (or size required
  for gauge)
1 large safety pin

GAUGE
15 sts = 3½" in afghan st,
7 rows = 2" in afghan st
8 sc = 4" in crochet

STITCH GUIDE

sc 2 sts together decrease (sc2tog): draw up a lp in
each of next 2 sts, YO and draw through 3 lps on
hook: sc2tog made.

sc 3 sts tog decrease (sc3tog): draw up a lp in each
of next 3 sts, YO and draw through 4 lps on hook:
sc3tog made.

tr 2 sts tog decrease (tr2tog): Holding back last lp of
each st on hook, tr in each of next 2 sts, YO and draw
though all 3 lps on hook: tr2tog made.

tr 3 sts tog decrease (tr3tog): Holding back last lp of
each st on hook, tr in each of next 3 sts, YO and draw
through all 4 lps on hook: tr3tog made.

Instructions

Panel (make 6)
With afghan hook, using Color A, ch 15.

Following Afghan Stitch instructions on page 124,
work 235 rows. At end of last row, weave in ends.
Mark working side as right side.

Notes: *to help keep track of row count, tie a contrast piece
of yarn at edge of every 10th row.*

Piece will curl up as you work; you may wish to roll
work periodically and pin it up with a large safety pin.

Panel Sides

Row 1: With right side of one panel facing and long
edge at top, join B with crochet hook in first st at upper
right; ch 1, sc in each row along edge: 235 sc; ch 1,
turn.

Row 2: Working in BLO, sc in each sc, ch 1, turn.

Row 3: Working in BLO, *sc in first st, hdc in next st,
dc in next st, 3 tr in next st, dc in next st, hdc in next st;
rep from * across, ending with sc in the last st. Finish
off B.

Row 4: With right side facing, attach C in last st made
in Row 3; sc2tog; *sc in next 2 sts, 3 sc in next st (middle st of 3 tr in row below), sc in next 2 sts, sc3tog; rep
from * across, ending last repeat with sc2tog; ch 1, turn.

Row 5: Working in BLO, rep Row 4; finish off.

Row 6: With right side facing, attach B at beginning of
row; working in BLO, ch 3, holding back last lp of st
on hook, work tr in next st, yo and draw through both
lps on hook; * dc in next st, hdc in next st, sc in next st,
hdc in next st, dc in next st, tr3tog; rep from * across,
ending last repeat with tr2tog in last st; ch 1, turn.

Rows 7 and 8: Working in BLO, sc in each st, ch 1,
turn; at end of Row 8, finish off. Weave in ends.

Turn piece so opposite long side is at top; work Rows
1 through 8 of Panel Sides.

Work crocheted sides on each rem panel.

Zig-Zag

Joining Panels

Hold two panels side by side with long edges tog and right side facing; join A with a sl st in first st at bottom of one panel, then sl st in same st on opposite panel; working loosely, continue joining by working sl sts in corresponding rows of each panel; at end, finish off.

Join all rem panels in same manner.

Edging

Row 1: Hold piece with right side facing; join A with sl st in any outer corner st, ch 1, 2 sc in same st (corner made); sc evenly around entire outer edge of afghan, working 2 sc for corner in each rem outer corner sp, and adjusting sts to keep work flat; join in beg sc, finish off.

Row 2: With B, rep Row 1, again adjusting sts to keep work flat. Finish off. Weave in ends.

knit
Romantic Lace

Designed by Patons Design Staff

SIZE
41" x 51"

MATERIALS
Worsted weight yarn,
 24 1/2 oz white
*Note: Photographed model made with Patons® Décor
 #1602 Aran*
29" Size 8 (5 mm) circular knitting needle (or size
 requirerd for gauge)
Size 8 (5 mm) double pointed needles
Stitch markers or small safety pints

GAUGE
18 sts = 4" in stockinette st (knit one row,
 purl one row)
24 rows= 4"

STITCH GUIDE

Sl 2 = insert needle from left to right into next 2 sts at same time and slip both sts.

P2SSO = pass 2 slipped sts over knit stitch

Instructions

Squares (make 20)

Note: Beg each square at outside edge with circular needle and switch to double-pointed needles as number of sts decreases.

CO 160 sts; join, place marker to indicate beg of rnd.

Rnd 1: *K19, sl 2, Kl, P2SSO (corner), K18; rep from * 3 times more: 152 sts.

Rnd 2: *P18, sl 2, Kl, P2SSO, P17; rep from * 3 times more: 144 sts.

Rnd 3: *Kl, (K2tog, YO) 8 times; sl 2, Kl, P2SSO, (K2tog, YO) 8 times; rep from * 3 times more: 136 sts.

Rnd 4: *P16, sl 2, Kl, P2SSO, P15; rep from * 3 times more: 128 sts.

Rnd 5: *K5, YO, sl 1, Kl, PSSO, K3, K2tog, YO, K3, sl 2, Kl, P2SSO; K3, YO, sl 1, Kl, PSSO, K3, K2tog, YO, K4; rep from * 3 times more: 120 sts.

Rnd 6: *K14; sl 2, Kl, P2SSO, K13; rep from * 3 times more: 112 sts.

Rnd 7: *Kl, YO, sl 1, Kl, PSSO, K3, YO, sl 1, Kl, PSSO, Kl, K2tog, YO, K2; sl 2, Kl, P2SSO; K2, YO, sl 1, Kl, PSSO, Kl, K2tog, YO, K3, K2tog, YO; rep from * 3 times more. 104 sts.

Rnd 8: *K12, sl 2, K1, P2SSO, Kl 1; rep from * 3 times more: 96 sts.

Rnd 9: *Kl, YO, Kl, sl 1, Kl, PSSO; K3, YO, sl 2, Kl, P2SSO, YO, Kl; sl 2, Kl, P2SSO; K1, YO, sl 2, Kl, P2SSO, YO, K3, K2tog, K1, YO; rep from * 3 times more: 88 sts.

Rnd 10: *K10, sl 2, Kl, P2SSO, K9; rep from * 3 times more: 80 sts.

Rnd 11: *Kl, YO, K2, sl 1, Kl, PSSO, K4; sl 2, Kl, P2SSO; K4, K2tog, K2, YO; rep from * 3 times more: 72 sts.

Rnd 12: *K8; sl 2, Kl, P2SSO; K7; rep from * 3 times more. 64 sts.

Rnd 13: *K3, K2tog, YO, K2; sl 2, Kl, P2SSO; K2, YO, sl 1, Kl, PSSO, K2; rep from * 3 times more: 56 sts.

Rnd 14: *K6; sl 2, Kl, P2SSO; K5; rep from * 3 times more: 48 sts.

Rnd 15: *K2, K2tog, YO, Kl, sl 2, Kl, P2SSO; Kl, YO, sl 1, Kl, PSSO, Kl; rep from * 3 times more: 40 sts.

Rnd 16: *K4; sl 2, Kl, P2SSO, K3; rep from * 3 times more: 32 sts

Rnd 17: *Kl, K2tog; YO, sl 2, Kl, P2SSO, YO, sl 1, Kl, PSSO; rep from * 3 times more: 24 sts.

Rnd 18: *K2; sl 2, Kl, P2SSO; Kl; rep from * 3 times more: 16 sts.

Delicate squares knitted from the outside in are interesting to create. A textured border is worked separately. Together the squares and border create a spectacular romantic throw that says to the recipient, "You are truly a special person,"

Rnd 19: *Kl, sl 2, Kl, P2SSO; rep from * 3 times more: 8 sts.

Cut yarn, thread into a yarn needle and draw through rem sts; fasten securely.

Finishing

Pin squares flat to shape and using a damp cloth, steam lightly, holding iron above square. Remove pins when thoroughly dry. Sew squares into 4 strips of 5 squares each, then sew strips tog.

Edging

With 2 double pointed needles, CO 17 sts.

Foundation

Row 1: Kl, YO, sl 1, Kl, PSSO, Kl, K2tog, YO, K7, YO, K2tog, K2.

Row 2: P3, YRN, P2tog; purl to end of row.

Body

Row 1: Kl, YO, K2tog, YO, K3, YO; sl 1, Kl, PSSO, K5, YO, K2tog, K2: 18 sts.

Row 2 and all even rows: P3, YRN, P2tog; purl to end of row.

Row 3: Kl, YO, K2tog,YO, K5, YO; sl 1, Kl, PSSO, K4, YO, K2tog, K2:19 sts.

Row 5: Kl, YO, K2tog, YO, K3, YO, sl 1, Kl, PSSO, K2, YO, sl 1, Kl, PSSO, K3, YO, K2tog, K2: 20 sts.

Row 7: Kl, YO, K2tog, YO, K3, (YO, sl 1, K1, PSSO) twice; K2, YO, sl 1, K1, PSSO, K2, YO, K2tog, K2: 21 sts.

Row 9: Kl, YO, K2tog, YO, K3, (YO, sl 1, K1, PSSO) 3 times, K2, YO, sl 1, K1, PSSO, Kl, YO, K2tog, K2: 22 sts.

Row 11: Sl 1, Kl, PSSO, (YO, sl 1, K1, PSSO) twice, K2, (YO, sl 1, Kl, PSSO) twice; Kl, K2tog, YO, K3, YO, K2tog, K2: 21 sts.

Row 13: Sl 1, Kl, PSSO, (YO, sl 1, Kl, PSSO) twice; K2, YO, sl 1, Kl, PSSO, Kl, K2tog, YO, K4, YO, K2tog, K2: 20 sts.

Row 15: Sl 1, Kl, PSSO, (YO, sl 1, Kl, PSSO) twice, K3, K2tog, YO, K5, YO, K2tog, K2: 19 sts.

Row 17: Sl 1, Kl, PSSO, (YO, sl 1, Kl, PSSO) twice, Kl, K2tog, YO, K6, YO, K2tog, K2: 18 sts.

Row 19: Sl 1, Kl, PSSO, YO, sl 1, Kl, PSSO, Kl, K2tog, YO, K7, YO, K2tog, K2: 17 sts.

Row 20: Rep Row 2.

Rep last 20 rows until edging from CO edge measures sufficient length to fit around outer edge, gathering at corners, ending with a 20th row of patt; BO.

Beg at center of one side edge, sew edging to afghan, gathering at each corner. Sew ends of edging tog. Using a damp cloth, steam edging and seams of squares lightly.

*Two of the knitter's favorite patterns – cables and lace –
combined in this most luxurious afghan made of cashmere
yarns make this a special gift for a very special person.*

knit
Wrapped in Cashmere

Designed by Sheila Jones

SIZE
48"x 60"

MATERIALS
Worsted weight yarn,
  3696 yards, 1200grams
Note: *Photographed model made with Plymouth Royal
  Cashmere # 8001*
32" Size 8 (5.0 mm) circular knitting needle (or size
  required for gauge)
Cable Needle

GAUGE
23 st= 4" measured over Pattern

STITCH GUIDE

Pattern (worked over 23 sts)

Row 1 (right side): K2, P1, K1, K2tog, YO, K1, YO,
SSK, K1, P1, K2, P1, K8 (cable stitches), P1.

Row 2 (wrong side): K1, P8 (cable stitches), K1, P2,
K1, P7, K1, P2.

Row 3: K2, P1, K2tog, YO, K3, YO, SSK, P1, K1, P1,
K8 (cable stitches), P1.

Row 4: Rep Row 2.

Continue working as for Rows 1 through 4, twisting cable
stitches on ninth row, then every tenth row thereafter.

Cable Twist: Sl the next 4 stitches to cable needle and
hold in front of work, knit the next 4 sts, then knit the
4 sts from cable needle: Cable Twist made.

Slip, slip, knit (SSK): Sl next 2 sts as to knit ; insert
tip of left needle into fronts of these 2 st and knit them
tog: SSK made

Instructions
Starting at lower edge, CO 278 sts.

Border
Rows 1 through 12: Knit.

Afghan Body

Row 1 (right side): K6; * K2, P1, K1, K2tog, YO, K1,
YO, SSK, K1, P1, K2, P1, K8 (cable sts), P1; rep from*
10 times more; K2, P1, K1, K2tog, YO, K1, YO, SSK,
K1, P1, K8.

Row 2 (and all wrong-side rows): K6; *P2, K1, P7,
K1, P2, K1, P8, K1; rep from * 10 times more; P2, K1,
P7, K1, P2, K6.

Row 3: K6; *K2, P1, K2tog, YO, K3, YO, SSK, P1, K2,
P1, K8, P1; rep from * 10 times more; K2, P1, K2tog,
YO, K3, YO, SSK, P1, K8.

Row 5: K6; * K2, P1, K1, K2tog, YO, K1, YO, SSK, K1,
P1, K2, P1, K8, P1; rep from* 10 times more; K2, P1,
K1, K2tog, YO, K1, YO, SSK, K1, P1, K8.

Row 7: K6; *K2, P1, K2tog, YO, K3, YO, SSK, P1, K2,
P1, K8, P1; rep from * 10 times more; K2, P1, K2tog,
YO, K3, YO, SSK, P1, K8.

Row 9 (Cable Twist row): K6; * K2, P1, K1, K2tog,
YO, K1, YO, SSK, K1, P1, K2, P1, Cable Twist, P1; rep
from * 10 times more; K2, P1, K1, K2tog, YO, K1, YO,
SSK, K1, P1, K8.

Row 10: Rep Row 2.

Rep Rows 1 through 10 until piece measures 58½"
from cast-on row, ending by working a right-side row,

Top Border

Knit 13 rows garter stitch, ending on wrong side.

BO loosely keeping the same tension as CO edge.

Weave in ends.

Fringe

Following Fringe Instructions on page 127, cut fringe
12" long and use three strands in each knot. Work
Single Knot Fringe, spacing knots 2" apart.

The play of light and shadows on the dimensional bells rings in an unusual and beautiful afghan which is knitted in blocks. The soft lilac shade of the yarn we chose has universal appeal, but you can make it in any favorite color.

The Sweet Sound of Bells

Designed by Nazanin S. Fard

SIZE
64" x 56"

MATERIALS
Worsted weight yarn,
  49 oz lilac
Note: *Photographed model made with Bernat® Berella® "4" #8712 Lilac Petal*
Size 7 (4.5 mm) knitting needles (or size required for gauge)
Size G (4 mm) crochet hook

GAUGE
16 sts = 4" in stockinette st (knit one row, purl one row)
Square = 8"

STITCH GUIDE

SL(sl): Slip next stitch as to knit with yarn in back.

SL P1 (sl P1): Slip next stitch as to purl with yarn in front.

LOOP CAST-ON (LCO): Lp yarn around left thumb, insert right needle into lp as if to knit, sl lp off thumb and onto needle: LCO made.

SSK: Sl next 2 stitches as if to knit, move them back to left needle (2nd st is now first), knit both tog through back lps.

SSP: Sl next 2 stitches as if to knit, move them back to left needle, purl both tog through back lps.

PSSO: Pass slipped stitch over stitch(es) just worked.

Instructions

Block (make 56)
Note: *Blocks are worked diagonally, starting at one corner*
CO 1 st.

Row 1: Knit in front and back of st: 2 sts.

Row 2: K2.

Row 3: Sl P1, LCO1, P1: 3 sts.

Row 4: Sl 1, K2.

Row 5: Sl P1, (LCO1, P1) 2 times: 5 sts.

Row 6: Sl 1, k4.

Row 7: Sl P1, LCO1, P3, LCO 1, P1: 7 sts.

Row 8: Sl 1, K6.

Row 9: Sl P1, LCO1, P2, LCO6, P2tog, P1, LCO1, P1: 14 sts.

Row 10: Sl 1, K3, P6, K4.

Row 11: Sl P1, LCO1, P3, SSK, K2, K2tog, P3, LCO1, P1: 14 sts.

Row 12: Sl 1, K4, P4, K5.

Row 13: Sl P1, LCO1, P4, SSK, K2tog, P4, LCO1, P1: 14 sts.

Row 14: Sl 1, K5, P2, K6.

Row 15: Sl P1, LCO1, P5, SSK, P5, LCO1, P1: 15 sts.

Row 16: Sl 1, K14.

Row 17: Sl P1, LCO1, P3, LCO6, P2tog, P4, LCO6, P2tog, P2, LCO1, P1: 27 sts.

Row 18: Sl 1, K4, (P6, K5) twice.

Row 19: Sl P1, LCO1, P4, SSK, K2, K2tog, P5, SSK, K2, K2tog, P4, LCO1, P1: 25 sts.

Row 20: Sl 1, (K5, P4) twice, K6.

Row 21: Sl P1, LCO1, P5, (SSK, K2tog, P5) twice, LCO1, P1: 23 sts.

Row 22: Sl 1, K6, P2, K5, P2, K7.

Row 23: Sl P1, LCO1, P6, SSK, P5, SSK, P6, LCO1, P1: 23 sts.

Row 24: Sl 1, K22.

Row 25: Sl P1, LCO1, (P4, LCO6, P2tog) 3 times, P3, LCO1, P1: 40 sts.

Row 26: Sl 1, (K5, P6) 3 times, K6.

Row 27: Sl P1, LCO1, P5, (SSK, K2, K2tog, P5) 3 times, LCO1, P1: 36 sts.

Row 28: Sl 1, K6, (P4, K5) twice, P4, K7.

Row 29: Sl P1, LCO1, P6, (SSK, K2tog, P5) twice, SSK, K2tog, P6, LCO1, P1: 32 sts.

Row 30: Sl 1, K7, (P2, K5) twice, P2, K8.

Row 31: Sl P1, LCO1, P7, (SSK, P5) twice, SSK, P7, LCO1, P1: 31 sts.

Row 32: Sl 1, K30.

Row 33: Sl P1, LCO1, K29, LCO1, P1: 33 sts.

Row 34: Sl 1, (P2tog, YO) 15 times, P2.

Row 35: Sl 1, LCO1, K31, LCO1, K1: 35 sts.

Row 36: Sl P1, K34.

Row 37: Sl P1, LCO1, P 33, LCO1, P1: 37 sts.

Row 38: Sl 1, P36.

Row 39: Sl 1, LCO1, K4, (K2tog, YO, K6) 3 times, K2tog, YO, K5, LCO1, K1: 39 sts.

Row 40: Sl P1, P38.

Row 41: Sl 1, LCO1, K4, (K2tog, YO, K1, YO, SSK, K3) 3 times, K2tog, YO, K1, YO, SSK, K4, LCO1, K1: 41 sts.

Row 42: Sl P1, P40.

Row 43: Sl 1, LCO1, K4, (K2tog, YO, K3, YO, SSK, K1) 3 times, K2tog, YO, K3, YO, SSK, K4, LCO1, K1: 43 sts.

Row 44: Sl P1, P42.

Row 45: Sl 1, SSK, K2, K2tog, YO, (K5, YO, Sl 1, K2tog, PSSO, YO) 3 times, K5, YO, SSK, K2, K2tog, K1: 41 sts.

Row 46: Sl P1, P40.

Row 47: Sl 1, SSK, K2tog, YO, K7, (YO, SSK, K6) 3 times, YO, SSK, K2tog, K1: 39 sts.

Row 48: Sl P1, P38.

Row 49: Sl 1, SSP, P33, P2tog, P1: 37 sts.

Row 50: Sl 1, K36.

Row 51: Sl P1, SSK, (K2tog, YO) 15 times, K1, K2tog, K1: 35 sts.

Row 52: Sl P1, P34.

Row 53: Sl 1, SSP, P29, P2tog, P1: 33 sts.

Row 54: Sl 1, K32.

Row 55: Sl P1, SSP, P8, (LCO6, P2tog, P3) twice, LCO6, P2tog, P7, P2tog, P1: 46 sts.

Row 56: Sl 1, K9, (P6, K4) twice, P6, K10.

Row 57: Sl P1, SSP, P7, (SSK, K2, K2tog, P4) twice, SSK, K2, K2tog, P7, P2tog, P1: 38 sts.

Row 58: Sl 1, K8, (P4, K4) twice, P4, K9.

Row 59: Sl P1, SSP, P6, (SSK, K2tog, P4) twice, SSK, K2tog, P6, P2tog, P1: 30 sts.

Row 60: Sl 1, K7, (P2, K4) twice, P2, K8.

Row 61: Sl P1, SSP, P5, (SSK, P4) twice, SSK, P5, P2tog, P1: 25 sts.

Row 62: Sl 1, K24.

Row 63: Sl P1, SSP, P7, LCO6, P2tog, P2, LCO6, P2tog, P6, P2tog, P1: 33 sts.

Row 64: Sl 1, K8, P6, K3, P6, K9.

Row 65: Sl P1, SSP, P6, SSK, K2, K2tog, P3, SSK, K2, K2tog, P6, P2tog, P1: 27 sts.

Row 66: Sl 1, K7, P4, K3, P4, K8.

Row 67: Sl P1, SSP, P5, SSK, K2tog, P3, SSK, K2tog, P5, P2tog, P1: 21 sts.

Row 68: Sl 1, K6, P2, K3, P2, K7.

Row 69: Sl P1, SSP, P4, SSK, P3, SSK, P4, P2tog, P1: 17 sts.

Row 70: Sl 1, K16.

Row 71: Sl P1, SSP, P5, LCO6, P2tog, P4, P2tog, P1: 20 sts.

Row 72: Sl 1, K6, P6, K7.

Row 73: Sl P1, SSP, P4, SSK, K2, K2tog, P4, P2tog, P1: 16 sts.

Row 74: Sl 1, K5, P4, K6.

Row 75: Sl P1, SSP, P3, SSK, K2tog, P3, P2tog, P1: 12 sts.

Row 76: Sl 1, K4, P2, K5.

Row 77: Sl P1, SSP, P2, SSK, P2, P2tog, P1: 9 sts.

Row 78: Sl 1, K8.

Row 79: Sl P1, SSP, P3, P2tog, P1: 7 sts.

Row 80: Sl 1, K6.

Row 81: Sl P1, SSP, P1, P2tog, P1: 5 sts.

Row 82: Sl 1, K4.

Row 83: Sl P2, P2tog, PSSO (2nd st only), P1: 3 sts.

Row 84: Sl 1, K2.

Row 85: Sl P1, SSP, PSSO: 1 st. Finish off.

Finishing

Sew blocks together following the diagram for placement. **Hint:** *Begin with a set of 4 blocks with the points going in the right directions to set the pinwheel shape in the middle.*

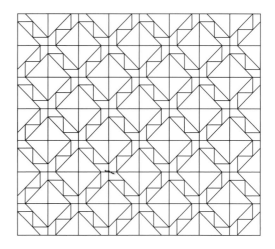

Border

Rnd 1: Hold piece with right side facing; with crochet hook, join yarn with sl st in upper right corner, ch 1, 3 sc in same place; work sc around entire outer edge, working 3 sc in each rem corner, and adjusting sts as needed to keep work flat.

Join with sl st in beg sc.

Rnd 2: Ch 1; working in reverse sc (work from left to right), sc in each sc around, working 3 sc in center sc of each corner 3-sc group; join; finish off; weave in ends.

*This is a striking afghan with masculine appeal. It's made in an unusual way...
first, you make the bottom end fringe; then you knit the body, then the fringe
for the top end – all in one piece. The color mixture gives a true tweed effect.*

knit
Tweed Treasure

designed by Cynthia Grosch

SIZE
40" x 60"

MATERIALS
Super bulky weight yarn,
  900 g (594 yds) white
  700 g (462 yds) grey
Note: *Photographed model made with Reynolds Blizzard Alpaca # 610 White; and #643 Grey*
29" Size 15 (10 mm) circular knitting needle
  (or size required for gauge)

GAUGE
21 sts = 8" in patt

STITCH GUIDE

Knitted Cast On: Make a sl knot on needle for first st; insert needle in st and knit, sl new st back on left needle; *insert needle in last st, and knit, sl new st back on left needle; rep from *.

Yarn in front (YF): Take yarn to front as to purl.

Yarn in back (YB): Take yarn to back as to knit

Tweed Pattern

Row 1: With white, *K1, YF, sl 1 as to purl, YB; rep from * across to last st, K1.

Row 2: P 2, *YB, sl 1 as to purl, YF, P1; rep from * across, purl in last st.

Rows 3 and 4: Change to grey and rep Rows 1 and 2.

Rep Rows 1 through 4 for pattern.

Notes

1. When changing colors, do not cut yarn; carry yarn not in use loosely up side.

2. Circular needle is used to accommodate large number of sts; do not join, work back and forth in rows.

3. Afghan is made in one piece, starting with Bottom Fringe, continuing with body, and ending with Top Fringe.

Instructions

Bottom Fringe

With white, using the knitted cast-on method (see Stitch Guide) ,* CO 14 sts, BO 12 sts: one fringe made, one st remains on right needle; sl this st as to purl back to left needle; rep from * until there are 34 fringes: 101 sts rem.

Body

Following Tweed Pattern and working on the 101 sts, rep Rows 1 through 4 until afghan measures 60", ending by working a Row 2; cut grey.

Top Fringe

Continuing with white,* CO 12 sts, bind off 14 sts; sl (as to purl) rem st on right needle to left needle; rep from * across, ending cast on 12 sts, BO 14 sts: 34 fringes made.

Weave in yarn ends.

Great in garter stitch, the combination of
colors in this afghan is unusual and appealing.
The off-set strips are easy and fun to knit, and
create the look of a patchwork quilt. This
colorway has masculine appeal, but in other
colors could be distinctly feminine.

knit
A Riot of Color

Designed by Patons Design Staff

SIZE
52" x 62"

MATERIALS
Worsted weight yarn,
  $3\frac{1}{2}$ oz black(MC)
  7 oz red (A)
  $3\frac{1}{2}$ oz navy (B)
  7 oz brown (C)
  7 oz juniper (D)
  $3\frac{1}{2}$ oz grey (E)
  $10\frac{1}{2}$ oz off white (F)
  7 oz gold (G)
  $3\frac{1}{2}$ oz blue (H)
  $10\frac{1}{2}$ oz orange (J)
  $3\frac{1}{2}$ oz purple (K)
Note: *Photographed model made with Patons®*
Canadiana #3 Black (MC), #5 Cardinal Red (A), #34
Navy (B), #107 Earth Brown (C), #54 Dk Juniper (D),
#311 Med Grey Heather (E), #104 Aran (F), #81 Gold
(G), #140 Dk Periwinkle (H), #72 Deep Orange (J),
and #151 Eggplant (K)
Size 8 (5 mm) knitting needles (or size required
  for gauge)

GAUGE
18 sts = 4" in garter st (knit every row)
34 rows = 4" in garter st

Instructions

Strip 1 (make 5)
With D, CO 26 sts.

Row 1: Knit; mark this row for wrong side.

Rows 2 through 49: Knit.

With F, knit 4 rows.

With D, knit 2 rows.

Rep last 6 rows once more.

With F, knit 50 rows.

With J, knit 4 rows.

With F, knit 2 rows.

With J, knit 50 rows.

With A, knit 4 rows.

With J, knit 2 rows.

Rep last 6 rows once more.

With A, knit 50 rows.

With MC, knit 4 rows.

With A, knit 2 rows.

Rep last 6 rows once more.

With G, knit 50 rows.

With K, knit 4 rows.

With J, knit 2 rows.

With K, knit 50 rows.

With C, knit 4 rows.

With K, knit 2 rows.

Rep last 6 rows once more.

With C, knit 50 rows.

With J, knit 4 rows.

With C, knit 2 rows.

With J, knit 50 rows.

With F, knit 4 rows.

With J, knit 2 rows.

Rep last 6 rows once more.

With F, knit 49 rows.

BO as to knit.

A Riot of Color

Strip 2 (make 4)

With A, CO 26 sts.

Row 1: Knit; mark this row as wrong side.

Rows 2 through 49: Knit.

With B, knit 4 rows.

With A, knit 2 rows.

Rep last 6 rows once more.

With B, knit 50 rows.

With C, knit 4 rows.

With B, knit 2 rows.

With C, knit 50 rows.

With D, knit 4 rows.

With C, knit 2 rows.

Rep last 6 rows once more.

With D, knit 50 rows.

With E, knit 4 rows.

With F, knit 2 rows.

Rep last 6 rows once more.

With E, knit 50 rows.

With F, knit 4 rows.

With E, knit 2 rows.

With F, knit 50 rows.

With MC, knit 4 rows.

With F, knit 2 rows.

Rep last 6 rows once more.

With MC, knit 50 rows.

With G, knit 4 rows.

With MC, knit 2 rows.

With G, knit 50 rows.

With H, knit 4 rows.

With G, knit 2 rows.

Rep last 6 rows once more.

With H, knit 49 rows.

BO as to knit.

Assembly

Sew strips tog alternating Strip 1 with Strip 2, beg and ending with Strip 1. Be sure all right sides are facing the same way; sew with yarn to match each patch color.

crochet
Pineapple Cream

SIZE
50" x 66"

MATERIALS
Worsted weight yarn,
  31 oz off white
*Note: Photographed model made with Red Heart®
  Super Saver® #313 Aran*
Size J (6 mm) crochet hook (or size required
  for gauge)

GAUGE
Motif = 16" across

STITCH GUIDE

Cluster (CL): (YO, insert hook in specified st,
YO and draw up a lp, YO and draw through 2 lps
on hook) 2 times, YO and draw through all 3 lps
on hook: CL made.

Beg cluster (beg CL): Ch 2, dc in joining: beg CL
made.

Corner group: (2 dc, ch 3, 2 dc) in specified ch lp: corner group made.

Tr decrease (tr dec): *YO twice, insert hook in next
ch-3 lp, YO and draw up a lp, (YO and draw through 2
lps on hook) twice; rep from * 3 times more, YO and
draw through all 5 lps on hook: tr dec made.

Picot: Sl st in specified st, ch 2, sl st in 2nd ch from
hook, sl st in same st: picot made.

Working around post: Insert hook from front to back
to front around specified st.

Instructions

First Motif

Ch 8; join with sl st to form a ring.

Rnd 1: Ch 4 (counts as tr), 27 tr in ring: 28 tr; join with
sl st in 4th ch of beg ch-4.

Rnd 2: Ch 5; *tr in next tr, ch 1; rep from * around: 28
tr and 28 ch-1 sps; join with sl st in 4th ch of beg ch-5.

Rnd 3: (Sl st, ch 1, sc) in first ch-1 sp; *ch 3, sc in next
ch-1 sp; rep from * around, ch 1, join with hdc in first
sc to form last 1p: 28 lps.

Rnd 4: Ch 2, dc around hdc post; *ch 3, skip next
2 ch-3 lps, 9 dc in next ch-3 lp, ch 3, skip next 2 ch-3
lps; CL in next ch-3 lp; ch 3**, CL in next ch-3 lp;
rep from * around, end at **; skip beg ch 2, join with
sl st in next dc.

Rnd 5: Beg CL, *ch 3, (tr in next dc, ch 1) 8 times,
tr in next dc**; (ch 3, CL in next CL) twice; rep from
* around, end at **; ch 3, CL in next CL, ch 3; join with
sl st in top of beg CL.

Rnd 6: Beg CL, *(ch 3, sc in next ch-1 sp) 8 times, ch 3,
CL in next CL, ch 5**, CL in next CL; rep from *
around, end at **; join as before.

Rnd 7: Beg CL, *ch 3, skip next ch-3 lp, (sc in next ch-
3 lp, ch 3) 7 times; CL in next CL, ch 3, corner group in
next ch-5 lp; ch 3**, CL in next CL; rep from * around,
end at **; join.

Rnd 8: Beg CL, *ch 3, skip next ch-3 lp, (sc in next
ch-3 lp, ch 3) 6 times; CL in next CL, ch 3, dc in next
2 dc, corner group in next ch-3 lp; dc in next 2 dc,
ch 3**, CL in next CL; rep from * around, end at **; join.

Rnd 9: Beg CL, *ch 3, skip next ch-3 lp, (sc in next
ch-3 lp, ch 3) 5 times; CL in next CL, ch 3, dc in next
4 dc, corner group in next ch-3 lp, dc in next 4 dc, ch
3**, CL in next CL; rep from * around, end at **; join.

Rnd 10: Beg CL, *ch 8, tr dec in next 4 ch-3 lps, ch 8,
CL in next CL, ch 3; dc in next 4 dc, ch 3, skip next 2
dc, corner group in next ch-3 lp, ch 3, skip next 2 dc, dc
in next 4 dc, ch 3**, CL in next CL; rep from * around,
end at **; join.

Rnd 11: Ch 1, *(sc, ch 5, sc) in next ch lp, ch 5; rep
from * around: 56 ch-5 lps; join with sl st in first sc.
Finish off and weave in ends.

Great for a pie — but also for an afghan, pineapples and cream are combined in this light and lovely creation. The traditional pineapple is rendered in an open version worked in squares with a picot border.

Second Motif

Rnds 1 through 10: Rep Rnds 1 through 10 on First Motif.

Rnd 11 (joining rnd): Ch 1, ((sc, ch 5, sc) in next ch lp, ch 5) 4 times; join side of 2 motifs as follows: sc in corner ch lp, ch 2, with wrong sides together sl st in corresponding corner ch lp on First Motif, *ch 2, sc in same ch lp on Second Motif, ch 2, sl st in next ch lp on First Motif, ch 2, sc in next ch lp on Second Motif, ch 2, sl st in next ch lp on First Motif; rep from * to next corner ch lp; ch 2, sc in corner ch lp on Second Motif, ch 2, sl st in corner ch lp on First Motif, ch 2, sc in same corner ch lp on Second Motif: one side joined; ch 5, complete same as for Rnd 11 on First Motif beginning at *. Finish off and weave in ends.

Make 3 rows of 4 motifs, joining motifs as before, joining on 2 sides where appropriate, and joining corners to previous corner joining (where 3 or 4 corners meet, sl st in previous joining sl st).

Border

Rnd 1: With right side facing, join with sl st in any of 4 outer corner ch lps; ch 3, 4 dc in same ch lp; *3 dc in each ch-5 lp to next corner**, 5 dc in corner ch-5 lp; rep from * around, end at **; join with sl st in 3rd ch of beg ch-3.

Rnd 2: Ch 1, sc in same ch as joining, sc in next dc, picot in next dc; *sc in next 3 dc, picot in next dc, **sc in next 2 dc, picot in next dc; rep from ** to next corner***; sc in next 2 dc, picot in next dc (center dc of corner 5 dc); rep from * to last st, end at ***; sc in next dc; join with sl st in first sc. Finish off and weave in ends.

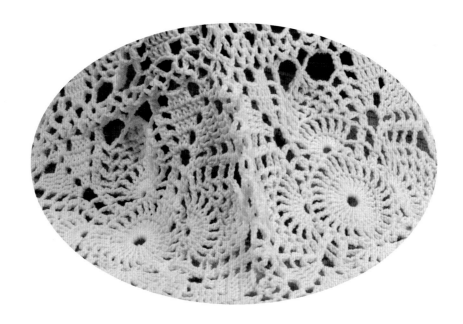

Honor a special person with your finest crochet work embodied in this one-of-a kind heirloom afghan. Lavish roses, which look as though they were carved from fine Ivory, display their open petals between bands of cables.

Carved Ivory Roses

designed by Mary Jane Protus for Coats and Clark
for the advanced crocheter

SIZE
46½" x 66"

MATERIALS
Worsted weight yarn,
  61 oz off white
Note: Photographed model made with Red Heart®
  Super Saver® #313 Aran
Size K (6.5 mm) crochet hook (or size required
  for gauge)
Size H (5 mm) crochet hook

GAUGE
23 sts = 8" in patt with larger hook
8 rows = 4" in patt with larger hook

STITCH GUIDE

Back Post dc (BPdc): YO, insert hook from back to front to back around post of next st, YO and draw up a lp, (YO and draw through 2 lps on hook) twice: BPdc made.

Front Post dc (FPdc): YO, insert hook from front to back to front around post of next st, YO and draw up a lp, (YO and draw through 2 lps on hook) twice: FPdc made.

Front Post tr (FPtr): YO twice, insert hook from front to back to front around post of specified st, YO and draw up a lp, (YO and draw through 2 lps on hook) 3 times: FPtr made.

Cross 2 left (C2L): Skip next st, FPdc in next st, FPdc in skipped st: C2L made.

Cross 6 left (C6L): Skip next 3 sts, FPtr in next 3 sts, working in front of last 3 FPtr, FPtr in 3 skipped sts: C6L made.

Cross 6 right (C6R): Skip next 3 sts, FPtr in next 3 sts, working behind last 3 FPtr, FPtr in 3 skipped sts: C6R made.

Triple Triple crochet (trtr): YO hook 4 times, insert hook in specified st and draw up a lp, (YO and draw through 2 lps) 5 times: trtr made.

3-dc group: 3 dc in sp between next 2 dc-groups.

Cable Row 1: BPdc in next st, C2L in next 2 sts, BPdc in next 2 sts, C6L in next 6 sts, FPdc in next 3 sts, BPdc in next 2 sts, C2L in next 2 sts, BPdc in next st: Cable Row 1 made.

Cable Row 2: FPdc in next st, BPdc in next 2 sts, FPdc in next 2 sts, BPdc in next 9 sts, FPdc in next 2 sts, BPdc in next 2 sts, FPdc in next st: Cable Row 2 made.

Cable Row 3: BPdc in next st, C2L in next 2 sts, BPdc in next 2 sts, FPdc in next 3 sts, C6R in next 6 sts, BPdc in next 2 sts, C2L in next 2 sts, BPdc in next st: Cable Row 3 made.

Instructions
With larger hook, ch 137.

Foundation Row: Dc in 4th ch from hook and in each ch across (3 skipped chs at beg count as first dc): 135 dc; ch 2, turn.

Row 1 (right side): Skip first dc; Cable Row 1 on next 19 dc; *dc in next dc, skip next dc, (3 dc in next dc, skip next 2 dc) 11 times; 3 dc in next dc, skip next dc, dc in next dc, Cable Row 1 on next 19 dc; rep from * to last st, hdc in last st, ch 2, turn.

Row 2: Cable Row 2; *2 dc in next dc; (3-dc group worked in sp between 3-dc groups of previous row) 5 times, ch 7, trtr in sp between next 2 groups, ch 7; (3-dc group in next sp) 5 times; skip 3 dc, 2 dc in next dc, Cable Row 2; rep from * to last st, hdc in 2nd ch of ch-2; ch 2, turn.

Row 3: Cable Row 3; *dc in next dc, (3-dc group worked in sp before 3-dc group of previous row) 5 times, ch 7, sc in next ch-7 lp, sc in trtr, sc in next ch-7 lp, ch 7; (3-dc group in sp after 3-dc group of previous row) 5 times, skip next dc, dc in next dc, Cable Row 3; rep from * to last st; hdc in 2nd ch of ch-2: ch 2, turn.

Row 4: Cable Row 2; *2 dc in next dc, (3-dc group) 4 times, ch 7, sc in lp, sc in 3 sc, sc in lp, ch 7, (3-dc group) 4 times; skip 3 dc, 2 dc in next dc, Cable Row 2; rep from * to last st; hdc in 2nd ch of ch-2; ch 2, turn.

Row 5: Cable Row 1; *dc in next dc, (3-dc group) 4 times, ch 7, sc in lp, sc in 5 sc, sc in lp, ch 7; (3-dc group) 4 times, skip next dc, dc in next dc, Cable Row 1; rep from * to last st; hdc in 2nd ch of ch-2; ch 2, turn.

Row 6: Cable Row 2; *2 dc in next dc, (3-dc group) 3 times, ch 7, sc in lp, sc in 7 sc, sc in lp, ch 7, (3-dc group) 3 times; skip 3 dc, 2 dc in next dc, Cable Row 2; rep from * to last st; hdc in 2nd ch of ch-2; ch 2, turn.

Row 7: Cable Row 3; *dc in next dc, (3-dc group) 3 times, ch 7, sc in lp, sc in 9 sc, sc in lp, ch 7; (3-dc group) 3 times, skip next dc, dc in next dc, Cable Row 3; rep from * to last st; hdc in 2nd ch of ch-2; ch 2, turn.

Row 8: Cable Row 2, *2 dc in next dc, (3-dc group) twice, ch 7, sc in lp, sc in 11 sc, sc in lp, ch 7; (3-dc group) twice, skip 3 dc, 2 dc in next dc, Cable Row 2; rep from * to last st; hdc in 2nd ch of ch-2; ch 2, turn.

Row 9: Cable Row 1; *dc in next dc, (3-dc group) twice, ch 7, sc in lp, sc in 13 sc, sc in lp, ch 7; (3-dc group) twice, skip next dc, dc in next dc, Cable Row 1; rep from * to last st; hdc in 2nd ch of ch-2; ch 2, turn.

Row 10: Cable Row 2; *2 dc in next dc, 3-dc group, ch 7, sc in lp, sc in 15 sc, sc in lp, ch 7, 3-dc group, skip 3 dc, 2 dc in next dc, Cable Row 2; rep from * to last st; hdc in 2nd ch of ch-2; ch 2, turn.

Row 11: Cable Row 3; *dc in next dc, 3-dc group, ch 7, sc in lp, sc in 17 sc, sc in lp, ch 7, 3-dc group, skip next dc, dc in next dc, Cable Row 3; rep from * to last st; hdc in 2nd ch of ch-2; ch 2, turn.

Row 12: Cable Row 2; *2 dc in next dc, 3 dc in lp, ch 7, skip next sc, sc in next 17 sc, skip next sc, ch 7; 3 dc in lp, skip 3 dc, 2 dc in next dc, Cable Row 2; rep from * to last st; hdc in 2nd ch of ch-2; ch 2, turn.

Row 13: Cable Row 1; *dc in next dc, 3-dc group, 3 dc in lp, ch 7, skip next sc, sc in next 15 sc, skip next sc, ch 7; 3 dc in lp, 3-dc group, skip next dc, dc in next dc, Cable Row 1; rep from * to last st; hdc in 2nd ch of ch-2; ch 2, turn.

Row 14: Cable Row 2; *2 dc in next dc, 3-dc group, 3 dc in lp, ch 7, skip next sc, sc in next 13 sc, skip next sc, ch 7; 3 dc in lp, 3-dc group, skip 3 dc, 2 dc in next dc, Cable Row 2; rep from * to last st; hdc in 2nd ch of ch-2; ch 2, turn.

Row 15: Cable Row 3; *dc in next dc, (3-dc group) twice, 3 dc in lp, ch 7, skip next sc, sc in next 11 sc, skip next sc, ch 7; 3 dc in lp, (3-dc group) twice, skip next dc, dc in next dc, Cable Row 3; rep from * to last st; hdc in 2nd ch of ch-2; ch 2, turn.

Row 16: Cable Row 2; *2 dc in next dc, (3-dc group) twice, 3 dc in lp, ch 7, skip next sc, sc in next 9 sc, skip next sc, ch 7; 3 dc in lp, (3-dc group) twice, skip 3 dc, 2 dc in next dc, Cable Row 2; rep from * to last st; hdc in 2nd ch of ch-2; ch 2, turn.

Row 17: Cable Row 1; *dc in next dc, (3-dc group) 3 times, 3 dc in lp, ch 7, skip next sc, sc in next 7 sc, skip next sc, ch 7; 3 dc in lp, (3-dc group) 3 times, skip next dc, dc in next dc, Cable Row 1; rep from * to last st; hdc in 2nd ch of ch-2; ch 2, turn.

Row 18: Cable Row 2; *2 dc in next dc, (3-dc group) 3 times, 3 dc in lp, ch 7, skip next sc, sc in next 5 sc, skip next sc, ch 7; 3 dc in lp, (3-dc group) 3 times, skip 3 dc, 2 dc in next dc, Cable Row 2; rep from * to last st; hdc in 2nd ch of ch-2; ch 2, turn.

Row 19: Cable Row 3; *dc in next dc, (3-dc group) 4 times, 3 dc in lp, ch 7, skip next sc, sc in next 3 sc, skip next sc, ch 7; 3 dc in lp, (3-dc group) 4 times, skip next dc, dc in next dc, Cable Row 3; rep from * to last st; hdc in 2nd ch of ch-2; ch 2, turn.

Row 20: Cable Row 2; *2 dc in next dc, (3-dc group) 4 times, 3 dc in lp, ch 1, skip next sc, trtr in next sc, ch 1; 3 dc in lp, (3-dc group) 4 times, skip 3 dc, 2 dc in next dc, Cable Row 2; rep from * to last st; hdc in 2nd ch of ch-2; ch 2, turn.

Row 21: Cable Row 1; *dc in next dc, (3-dc group) 5 times, (3 dc in next ch-1 sp) twice, (3-dc group) 5 times;

skip next dc, dc in next dc, Cable Row 1; rep from * to last st; hdc in 2nd ch of ch-2; ch 2, turn.

Rows 22 through 121: Rep Rows 2 through 21 five times more.

Row 122: Ch 1, skip first st, dc in each st across, dec over cables as necessary to keep work flat, dc in 2nd ch of ch-2; ch 1, turn.

Border

Note: Change to smaller hook.

Rnd 1: 2 sc in first st (corner), sc evenly around having a multiple of 3 sts across each side, working 3 sc in each of next 3 corners, and work 1 more sc in first corner; join with sl st in first sc.

Rnd 2: Ch 4, 3 dc in same sc as joining, skip next 2 sc; *3 dc in next sc, skip next 2 sc; rep from * to next corner**, (3 dc, ch 1, 3 dc) in next sc (corner), skip next 2 sc; rep from * around, end at **; work 2 more dc in first sc; join with sl st in 3rd ch of ch-4.

Rnd 3: (Sl st, ch 4, 3 dc) in first ch-1 sp; *3-dc group in center dc of 3-dc group; rep from * to corner**, (3 dc, ch 1, 3 dc) in corner ch-1 sp; rep from * around, end at **; work 2 more dc in first ch-1 sp; join with sl st in 3rd ch of ch-4.

Rnd 4: Sl st in first sp, ch 1; *(sc, ch 5, sc) in corner sp, ch 5, **sc between next 2 groups, ch 5; rep from ** to corner; rep from * around; join with sl st in first sc.

Rnd 5: Sl st in next 3 chs, ch 1; *(sc, ch 5, sc) in corner lp, ch 5, **sc in next lp, ch 5; rep from ** to corner; rep from * around; join with sl st in first sc.

Rnd 6: Sl st in next 3 chs, ch 1; *(sc, ch 3, sc) in corner lp, ch 3, **sc in next lp, ch 3; rep from ** to corner; rep from * around; join with sl st in first sc.

Rnd 7: Ch 1, *(sc, dc, tr, dc, sc) in ch-3 lp; rep from * around; join with sl st in first sc. Finish off and weave in ends.

Flower (make 12)

With smaller hook, leaving a long end before beg slip knot, ch 18.

Row 1: Dc in 4th ch from hook (3 skipped chs count as first dc), 2 dc in each ch across: 30 dc; ch 1, turn.

Row 2: Sc in first dc, *ch 3, sc in next st; rep from * across. Finish off, leaving a long end. Sew short ends together. Thread yarn needle with beg yarn end, weave through sts of beg ch, pull tightly to gather and secure. Sew flower to center of diamond.

Diamonds are forever, and so is the wonderful afghan that will commemorate a special occasion for a special friend. The diamond shapes are set at an angle in open squares, creating an unusual and interesting pattern.

crochet
Diamond Lace

Designed by Patons Design Staff

SIZE
46" x 56"

MATERIALS
Worsted weight yarn,
  35 oz white
Note: *Photographed model made with Patons® Canadiana*
  #101 Winter White
Size I (5.50 mm) crochet hook (or size required
  for gauge)

GAUGE
16 dc = 4 ins

Instructions
Ch 211.

Foundation Row: Dc in 4th ch from hook and in
each rem ch: 209 dc; ch 4 (counts as first tr of following
row), turn.

Row 1: Tr in next st; *ch 4, skip next 3 sts, sc in next
st, ch 3, turn; 5 dc in ch-4 sp, ch 3, turn; skip first dc,
dc in each of next 4 dc, dc in 3rd ch of ch-3: diamond
made; skip next 3 dc, tr in each of next 2 dc; rep from
* across, working last tr in 4th ch of turning ch-4; ch 4
(counts as first tr of following row), turn.

Row 2: Tr in next tr; *ch 3, sc in 3rd ch at point of
next diamond of Row 1; ch 3, tr in each of next 2 tr;
rep from * across, working last tr in 4th ch of of turning
ch-4; ch 3, turn.

Row 3: Dc in next tr; *3 dc in next ch-3 sp, dc in next
sc, 3 dc in next ch-3 sp, dc in each of next 2 tr; rep
from * across, working last dc in top of turning ch;
ch 6, turn.

Row 4: Skip next 3 dc; * dc in each of next 3 dc, ch 3,
skip next 3 dc; rep from * across, dc in 3rd ch of turning ch; ch 3, turn.

Row 5: *3 dc in next ch-3 sp, ch 3, skip next 3 dc; rep
from * across, ending 3 dc in ch-6 sp, dc in 3rd ch of
ch-6; ch 6, turn.

Row 6: Skip next 3 dc; *3 dc in next ch-3 sp, ch 3, skip
next 3 dc; rep from * to last st, dc in 3rd ch of turning
ch; ch 3, turn.

Row 7: *3 dc in next ch-3 sp, dc in each of next 3 dc;
rep from * across, ending with 3 dc in ch 6 space, dc in
3rd ch of ch-6; ch 4, turn.

Rep Rows 1 through 7 until piece measures about 46",
ending by working a Row 3. Finish off; weave in ends.

First Side Border

Join yarn with a sl st at one corner on one short side
edge.

Row 1: Ch 3 (counts as first dc), work 181 dc evenly
along side edge; ch 4, turn.

Rows 2 through 4: Rep Rows 1 through 3 of pattern;
at end of last row, do not work turning ch; finish off.

Second Side Border

On opposite short edge, work same as First Side
Border; at end of last row, do not finish off.

Edging

Ch 3, work one rnd of dc around entire outer edge of
afghan, working 3 dc in each corner; join with a sl st in
3rd ch of beg ch-3; finish off; weave in ends.

Beautiful bouquets of delicate cross stitch flowers parade up this sweet afghan. Worked from a chart, this design is based on a vintage embroidery piece, and is even more beautiful worked as an afghan. The piece is worked in panels.

crochet
Flower Bouquet

designed by Rita Weiss

SIZE
48" x 62"

MATERIALS
Worsted weight yarn,
  48 oz off white
Note: *Photographed model made with TLC®*
Essentials™ #2313 Aran
Persian type wool needlepoint yarn (for embroidery),
  14 yds lt pink
  35 yds med pink
  21 yds dk pink
  7 yds very dk pink
  7 yds very lt green
  77 yds med green
  28 yds dk green
  7 yds lt yellow
  7 yds med yellow
  14 yds blue
  7 yds purple
Size J (6 mm) afghan hook (or size required for gauge)
Size J (6 mm) crochet hook
Size 18 tapestry needle (for embroidery)

GAUGE
4 sts and 3 rows =1" in afghan st

STITCH GUIDE
Afghan Stitch: Follow instructions on page 124.

Cross Stitch on Afghan Stitch: Follow instructions on page 124.

Instructions

Center Panel (make 1)
With afghan hook and worsted weight yarn, ch 58 loosely.

Work 195 rows in afghan st, following instructions on page 124. At end of last row, BO.

Use Chart 1 to embroider design on Center Panel.

Starting 9 rows from the top and placing 17 rows between each design, embroider three floral motifs.

Side Panel (make 4)
With afghan hook, ch 20 loosely.

Work 195 rows in afghan st, following instructions on page 124. At end of last row, BO.

Use Chart 2 to embroider design on Side Panels. Starting 9 rows from top, work design six times moving from top to bottom of panel. At end of panel, work from Chart 3.

Edging (worked on both sides of center panel and side panels)

Left Edging
Hold panel with right side facing, top (bound-off) edge at your right and side edge across top. Using crochet hook, join yarn with sl st in last BO st at upper right-hand corner.

Row 1: Ch 5, sk first 2 rows, hdc in next row; *ch 2, sk next 2 rows, hdc in next row; rep from * across, ending in last row at upper left-hand corner; ch 5, turn.

Row 2: *Hdc in next hdc, ch 2; rep from * across, ending with hdc in 3rd ch of ch-5. Finish off.

Right Edging
Hold same panel with right side facing and opposiste edge at top. Using crochet hook, join yarn with sl st in first row at upper right-hand corner.

Row 1: Ch 5, *sk next 2 rows, hdc in next row, ch 2; rep from * across ending hdc in first BO st at upper left-hand corner; ch 5, turn.

Row 2: Work same as Left Edging. Finish off, weave in ends.

Joining
Place panels side by side with right sides up, having Side Panels at each outside edge and Center Panel in

the middle. Join two panels by holding yarn at back of work and work sl sts on right side, alternating from edge to edge as follows. With crochet hook, join yarn with a sl st in st at bottom edge of right panel. Insert hook in corresponding st at bottom edge of left panel; hook yarn from beneath work and draw up through work and lp on hook: sl st made. Work sl st in next st on Right Panel; then work sl st in corresponding st on Left Panel. Cont working in this manner (alternating sl sts from edge to edge) until panels are joined; finish off. Join rem panels in same manner.

Fringe

Following fringe instructions on page 127, make triple knot fringe. Cut 25" strands and use 8 strands for each knot of fringe. Tie knots evenly space across each short end of afghan.

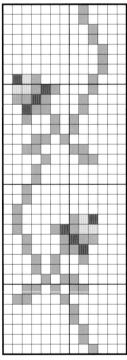

Chart 2

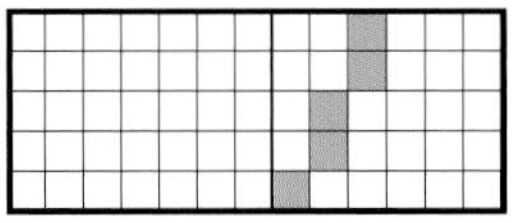

▨ light pink
▨ medium pink
▨ dark pink
▨ vry dark pink
▨ light green
▨ medium green
▨ dark green
  light yellow
▨ medium yellow
▨ blue
▨ purple

Chart 3

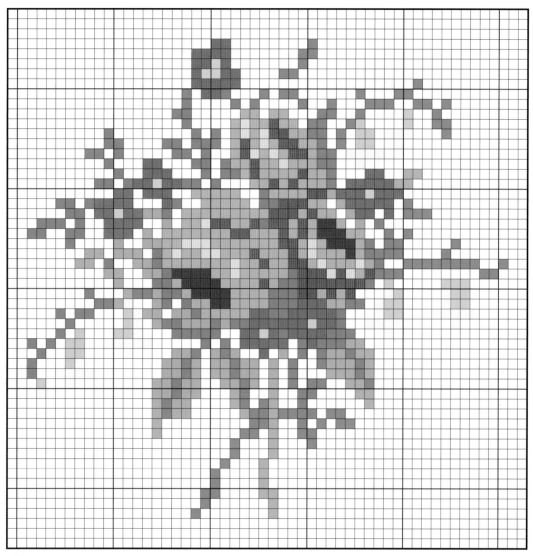

Chart 1

▓ light pink
▓ medium pink
▓ dark pink
▓ vry dark pink
▓ light green
▓ medium green
▓ dark green
  light yellow
▓ medium yellow
▓ blue
▓ purple

The tradition of Irish Crochet
is beautifully interpreted in
this magnificent lacy piece
worked in the traditional pure
white. Dimensional roses are
focal point of this exquisite
and very feminine afghan.

crochet
Irish Lace

Designed by Patons Design Staff

SIZE
56" x 64"

MATERIALS
Worsted weight yarn,
   63 oz white
*Note: Photographed model made with Patons®
   Canadiana #101 Winter White*
Size J (6 mm) crochet hook (or size required
   for gauge)

GAUGE
1 square = 4" x 4"

STITCH GUIDE

2 dc Cluster (2dcCL): Holding back last lp of each st,
work 2 dc in sp or st indicated, YO and draw through
all 3 lps on hook: 2dcCL made.

3 dc Cluster (3dcCL): Holding back last lp of each st,
work 3 dc in sp or st indicated, YO and draw through
all 4 lps on hook: 3dcCL made.

Instructions

Panel (make 7)

Square One
Ch 6, join with a sl st to form a ring.

Rnd 1: Ch 2, in ring work 2dcCL, ch 3; (in ring work
3dcCL, ch 3) 7 times, ch 3, join with sl st in top of beg
2dcCL: 8 CLs made.

Rnd 2: Sc in next ch-3 sp, (ch 5, sc in next ch-3 sp) 7
times, ch 5, dc in beg sc.

Rnd 3: In next ch-5 sp work (2dcCL, ch 3, 3dcCL) for
corner; *ch 5, sc in next ch-5 sp, ch 5, (3dcCL, ch 3,
3dcCL) in next ch-5 sp for corner; rep from * twice
more, ch 5, sc in next ch-5 sp, ch 5, join with sl st in
top of beg 2dcCL: four corners made; finish off; weave
in ends.

Squares Two through Fifteen
Rnds 1 and 2: Work as Square One.

*Note: On the following rnd, the new square will be joined
to a prev square.*

Rnd 3: Ch 5; * (3dcCL, ch 1) in next sp ; insert hook
from right side in center ch of corner of prev square
and sl st; (ch 1, 3dcCL) in same sp on new square *;
**ch 2, insert hook from right side in center ch of next
sp of prev square and sl st, ch 2**; sl st in next sp on
new square; rep from ** to ** once more, then rep from
* to * once more: 2 squares joined; [ch 5, sc in next sp,
ch 5; (3dcCL, ch 3, 3dcCL) in next sp] twice; ch 5, join
with sl st; finish off; weave in ends.

Panel Edging

Row 1: Join yarn with sl st in one corner ch-3 sp of
square at one end of panel; ch 3, 2 dc in same sp;
*(5 dc in next ch-5 sp) twice, 2 dc in corner ch-3 sp,
dc between squares (over joining st); 2 dc in next
corner sp; rep from * ending with 3 dc in last corner
ch-3 space; ch 3, turn.

Row 2: Skip first 2 dc, sc before first group of 5-dc of
prev row; *ch 5, sc between each 5-dc group; rep from
* to last 3-dc group, ch 3, sc in top of ch 3; ch 3, turn.

Row 3: 2 dc in ch-3 sp; *5 dc in next ch-5 sp; rep from
* to last ch-3 sp, 3 dc in sp, ch 3, turn.

Row 4: Skip first 2 sts; *(dc, ch 2, dc) in next st, skip
next 3 sts; rep from * to last 4 sts, (dc, ch 2, dc) in next
st, skip next 2 sts, dc in last st; ch 2, turn.

Row 5: Hdc in first dc; *hdc in ch-2 sp, hdc in next dc,
skip next dc; rep from * across, ending hdc in top of
ch-3; finish off; weave in ends.

Rep Panel Edging across opposite side of panel.

Joining

Hold two panels with right sides tog and sew tog through BLO of each hdc along edges. Join rem panels in same manner.

Fringe

Following Fringe Instructions on page 127 cut yarn into 24-inch lengths. Work Double Knot Fringe across each end of afghan, using 3 strands in outer knot at each end, and 6 strands in each rem knot.

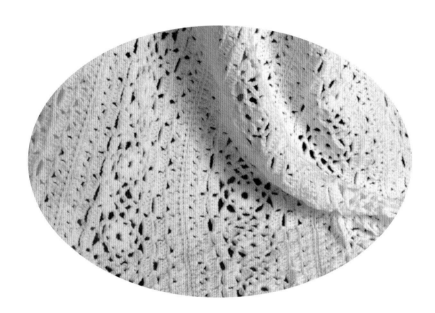

crochet
Blossoming Bullions

Designed by Bonnie Pierce

SIZE
45" x 57"

MATERIALS
Worsted weight yarn,
  32 oz off white
*Note: Photographed model made with Red Heart®
  Super Saver® # 313 Aran*
Size I (5.5 mm) crochet hook (or size required
  for gauge)
Size G (4 mm) crochet hook (for border)

GAUGE
10 sc = 3" with larger hook

STITCH GUIDE

Bullion Stitch

If you've never used the bullion stitch before, you'll want to practice it before starting the afghan. It takes some practice to be able to do it easily, but once you've mastered bullions, you'll find them fun to work and will love the interesting texture they add to your projects. Bullions are worked like an hdc, but with a lot more yarn overs.

To practice the bullion stitch, work this sample swatch with scrap yarn:

With worsted weight scrap yarn, ch 11.

Row 1: Sc in 2nd ch from hook and in each rem ch: 10 sc; ch 2 (counts as first hdc of following row), turn.

Row 2: YO, insert hook in next sc and draw up a lp; YO and draw through all 3 lps on hook: one hdc made.

For the next st, YO twice, insert hook in next sc and draw up a lp; YO and draw through all 4 lps on hook. (**Fig 1**)

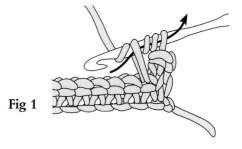

Fig 1

Try to draw the yarn through all 4 lps at once, but if necessary, you can use your fingers to pull the lps off one at a time: one 2-YO bullion st made.

For the next st, YO 3 times, insert hook in next sc and draw up a lp, YO and draw through all 5 lps at once; this will be a bit more difficult, but keep at it: one 3-YO bullion st made. (**Fig 2**)

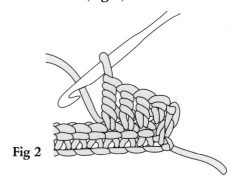

Fig 2

Continue in this manner across the row, adding one more YO at the beginning of each st, until you have 10 YOs . At end of row, ch 3, turn.

For this pattern, we use a 5-YO bullion for the rondels and a 10-YO bullion in the border, so continue working until you have mastered the stitch with 5 and 10 YOs in each. Take your time and pull the lps off by hand if necessary until you can do it in one sweeping motion.

Dimensional bullion stitch blossoms are made individually and then crocheted into a beautiful cover. The stunning border adds the perfect finishing touch to this challenging but rewarding afghan.

Instructions

Notes

1. First you will make all of the rondels used in the afghan; then they will be joined to the afghan body as you work it.

2. **Slip Knot Loop:** Begin as for a regular sl knot, but instead of drawing yarn up to make a tight lp on hook, leave a long lp into which you will work sts.

Rondel (make 248)

Make Slip Knot Lp; ch 2, working into lp, (5-YO bullion, ch 1) 10 times; tighten short end of yarn to close lp, finish off, weave in ends.

Body

With larger hook, ch 181.

Row 1: Sc in 2nd ch from hook and in each ch across: 180 sc; ch 1, turn.

Rows 2 through 4: Sc in each sc, ch 1, turn.

Row 5: Sc in first 5 sc; *hold right side of one rondel against working row (wrong side facing you); (insert hook through top of next bullion on rondel and through next sc on working row, YO and draw up a lp, YO and draw through 2 lps on hook: joining sc made) 5 times; sc in next 5 sc on working row; rep from * across, ending with sc in last 5 sts: 17 rondels joined; ch 1, turn.

Row 6: *Sc in next 5 sts; turn rondel up with right side now facing, sc in top of each rem 5 bullions on rondel; rep from * across row, ending with sc in last 5 sc; ch 1, turn.

Rows 7 through 14: Sc in each sc, ch 1, turn.

Row 15: Sc in first 10 sc; *hold right side of one rondel against working row as before; (insert hook through top of next bullion on rondel and through next sc on working row, YO and draw up a lp, YO and draw through 2 lps on hook: joining sc made) 5 times; sc in next 5 sc on working row; rep from * across, ending with sc in last 10 sts: 16 rondels joined; ch 1, turn.

Row 16: *Sc in next 10 sts; turn rondel up as before, sc in top of each rem 5 bullions on rondel, sc in next five sc; rep from * across, ending last rep sc in last 10 sc; ch 1, turn.

Rows 17 through 24: Sc in each sc, ch 1, turn.

Rep Rows 5 through 24 six times more, then rep Rows 5 through 14 once more.

Last 5 rows: Sc in each sc, ch 1, turn.

At end of last row, do not finish off yarn.

Edging

Rnd 1: Change to smaller hook; 3 sc in first st for corner; work sc evenly around afghan, adjusting sts to keep work flat, and working 3 sc in each corner; join in beg sc.

Rnd 2: *Ch 2, 10-YO bullion in next st, sl st in next 2 sts; rep from * around, join in beg bullion; finish off, weave in ends.

If you work on this soft green afghan on a winter day, you'll know Spring can't be far away. There is never a dull moment when knitting this wonderful piece: the cables and bobbles parade up and down under your skilled fingers.

knit
Springtime Favorite

Designed by Nazanin S. Fard

SIZE
64" x 56"

MATERIALS
Worsted weight yarn,
  52$\frac{1}{2}$ oz green
Note: *Photographed model made with Bernat® Berella®
  "4" #1232 Gentle Green*
Size 9 (5.5 mm) knitting needles (or size required
  for gauge)
36" Size 9 (5.5 mm) circular knitting needle
Cable needle
Size G (4 mm) crochet hook

GAUGE
16 sts = 4" in stockinette st (knit one row,
  purl one row)

STITCH GUIDE

C4F: Sl next 2 sts onto cable needle and hold in front,
purl next 2 sts from left needle, then knit 2 sts from
cable needle.

C4B: Sl next 2 sts onto cable needle and hold in back,
purl next 2 sts from left needle, then knit 2 sts from
cable needle.

K5TOG (K5tog): With yarn in front, sl 3 sts as if to
purl, K2tog, pass all 3 slipped sts over the K2tog.

M1: Knit into the back of the strand of yarn between
the stitch just worked and the next st.

M3: [K1, P1, K1] all in the same st.

3-needle bind off:

1. With the right side of both pieces facing each other,
hold both needles parallel in left hand. Insert the right
needle knitwise into the first 2 sts on both needles.

2. Wrap yarn around needle as if to knit and knit both
sts tog.

3. Knit the next 2 sts tog as described in Steps 1 and 2.

4. Sl the first st worked on to the right needle over the
second st just made to bind off.

5. Rep Steps 3-4 until all stitches are bound off.

Instructions
Note: *Sl all sts as to knit unless otherwise specified.*

Strip 1 (make 10):
CO 12 sts.

Rows 1 through 4: Knit.

Row 5 (right side): Sl 1 as to purl, P1, K2, P4, K2, P2.

Row 6: Sl 1, K1, P2, K4, P2, K2.

Row 7: Sl 1 as to purl, P1, C4F, C4B, P2.

Row 8: Sl 1, K1, P8, K2.

Rows 9 and 11: Rep Row 5.

Rows 10 and 12: Rep Row 6.

Rep Rows 5 through 12 until piece measures 60" from
CO edge

Knit 4 rows. BO all sts loosely.

Strip 2 (Make 9):
CO 19 sts.

Rows 1 through 4: Knit across.

Row 5 (right side): Sl 1 as to purl, K1, (P5, K1, P1, K1)
twice, P1 .

Row 6: Sl 1, P1, (K1, P1, K5, P1) twice, K1.

Row 7: Rep Row 5.

Row 8: Sl 1, P1, (M1, M3, M1, P1, K5tog, P1) twice,
K1.

Row 9: Sl 1 as to purl, K1, (P1, K1, P5, K1) twice; P1.

Row 10: Sl 1, P1, (K5, P1, K1, P1) twice, K1.

Rows 11 and 13: Rep Row 9.

Row 12: Rep Row 10.

Row 14: Sl 1, P1, (K5tog, P1, M1, M3, M1, P1) twice, K1.

Row 15: Rep Row 5.

Row 16: Rep Row 6.

Rep Rows 5 through 16 until piece measures 60" from CO edge.

Knit 4 rows. BO all sts loosely.

Joining:

Using circular needle, pick up one st for each slipped st along the edge of strip 1 and strip 2 and using the 3-needle bind off technique join the strips.

Finishing

Rnd 1: Hold piece with right side facing; with crochet hook, join yarn with sl st in upper right corner, ch 1, 3 sc in same place; work sc around entire outer edge, working 3 sc in each rem corner, and adjusting sts as needed to keep work flat.

Join with sl st in beg sc.

Rnd 2: Ch 1; working in reverse sc (work from left to right), sc in each sc around, working 3 sc in center sc of each corner 3-sc group; join, finish off, weave in ends.

knit
Black and White Diamonds

SIZE
42" x 63"

MATERIALS
Worsted weight yarn,
   24½ oz black (MC)
   24½ oz white (A)
Note: Photographed model made with Patons® Décor #1603 Black (MC) and #1614 Winter White
36" Size 7 (4 mm) circular knitting needle
   (or size for gauge)

GAUGE
20 sts = 4" in patt
32 rows = 4 ins in patt

STITCH GUIDE

KW = Knit, wrapping yarn twice around needle.

Sl 1P = Sl 1 st as to purl.

yb = bring yarn to back of work.

yf = bring yarn to front of work.

Instructions

With MC, cast on 210 sts. Do not join, work back and forth in rows.

Bottom Border

Row 1 (wrong side): Knit.

Rows 2 and 3: Rep Row 1.

Body

Row 1 (right side): Work first row of Chart on page 101, reading Row 1 from right to left

(*Note: 30-step rep is worked 7 times.*)

Row 2: Work Row 2 of Chart reading chart from left to right.

Row 3: Work Row 3 of Chart, reading chart from right to left.

Row 4: Work Row 4 of Chart, reading chart from left to right.

Continue working the remaining rows on the chart, working the odd-numbered rows from right to left and the even-numbered rows from left to right.

Work Rows 1 through 92 of chart 5 more times.

Top Border

Row 1 (right side): Knit

Rows 2 and 3: Knit

BO as if to knit.

Side Edgings

With right side of work facing and MC, pick up and knit 279 sts along one side edge of afghan. Knit 2 rows. BO as if to knit.

Rep on opposite side edge.

This afghan will be as cherished as a diamond! Worked from a chart that is easy to follow, the pattern is unusual and the result is wonderfully graphic.

Black and White Diamonds

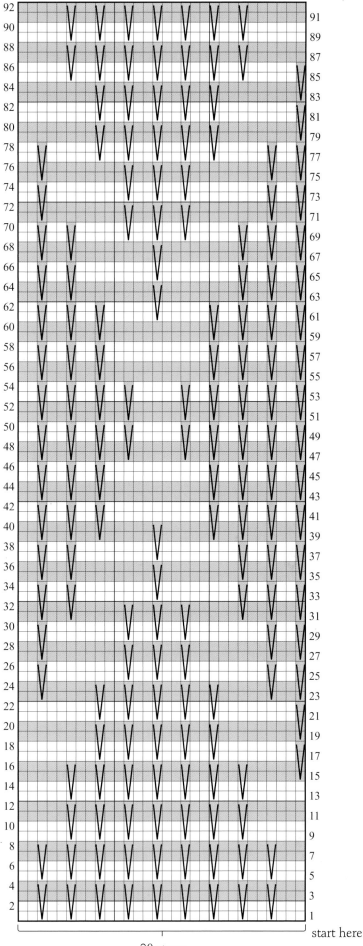

Key

☐ = MC, knit on right and wrong side rows.

⋁ = **1st row (right side):** With MC, KW.
2nd row: yf Sl1P (dropping extra loop)
3rd row: yb Sl1P
4th row: yf Sl1P

▨ = Contrast A, knit on right and wrong side rows.

⋁ = **1st row (right side):** With MC, KW.
2nd row: yf Sl1P (dropping extra loop)
3rd row: yb Sl1P
4th row: yf Sl1P

30 st rep

start here

The traditional afghan stitch is used to make the dimensional popcorns and chevrons that decorate this beautiful afghan. The special stitches really stand out against the flat background.

crochet
Chevron Popcorn

Designed by Patons Design Staff

SIZE
48" x 70"

MATERIALS
Worsted weight yarn,
  52½ oz off white
Note: *Photographed model made with Patons®Canadiana #104 Aran*
Size 6 (4 mm) afghan crochet hook (or size required
  for gauge)

GAUGE
17 sts = 4" in afghan stitch
14 rows = 4" in afghan stitch

STITCH GUIDE

Basic Afghan St: Follow instructions on page 124.

Bobble (BB): Ch 3, dc in 3rd ch from hook: BB made.

Popcorn (PC): 4 dc in specified st, remove hook from last st and insert in top of first dc of group, insert again in last dc and draw lp through: PC made.

Instructions

Panel (make 5)
Ch 24.

Rows 1 through 5: Work in Basic Afghan St.

Row 6: Pick up 24 sts; work off 12 lps; ch 3, dc in 3rd ch from hook: BB made; work off rem 12 lps.

Row 7: Pick up 24 sts; work off 11 lps, BB, work off 2 lps, BB, work of rem 10 lps.

Row 8: Rep Row 6.

Rows 1 through 8 of Chart on page 104 are now complete.

Now following chart, work Rows 9 through 75; then work Rows 12 through 75; then work Rows 12 through 53; then work Rows 1 through 13; finish off, weave in ends.

Border

Hold piece with right side facing.

Rnd 1: Join yarn in lower right-hand corner with sc; * working around entire outer edge, and starting along one side edge of panel work sc along edge to next corner, ch 1 for corner, work along next edge to corner, ch 1 for corner; rep from * around, join in beg sc.

Rnd 2: Ch 2, dc in next 2 sc; **PC in next st, dc in next 5 sts **; rep from ** to ** to 5 sts before next corner, PC in next st, dc in next 4 sts; skip corner ch-1 sp, ch 3 for corner, dc in next 4 sts; PC in next st (dc in next 5 sts, PC in next st) twice; dc in next 4 sts, sk ch-1 corner sp, ch 3; dc in next 4 sts; rep from ** to ** to last 4 sts before corner, PC in next st, dc in next 3 sts, skip ch-1 sp, ch 3, dc in next 4 sts, PC in next st; (dc in next 5 sts, PC in next st) twice; dc in next 4 sts, skip ch-1 sp, ch 3, join in top of beg ch-2.

Rnd 3: Ch 2, dc in next st; **[*skip next st, dc in next st, dc in skipped st: crossed dc made *; rep from * to * to 2 sts before corner, dc in each of next 2 sts; (skip next st, dc in next st, dc in skipped st) 9 times, 2 dc in next st; (2dc, ch 2, 2 dc) in next ch-3 sp]**; dc in next 2 sts; rep from ** to ** once more, join in beg ch-2.

Rnd 4: Ch 2; *working in back lp only of each st, dc in each st to corner ch; (dc, ch 2, dc) in corner ch-2 sp; rep from * around, join in beg dc; finish off; weave in ends.

Finishing

With right sides tog, sew panels tog.

Fringe

Following Fringe Instructions on page 127, cut 12" strands and work Single Knot Fringe, using 6 strands in each knot across short ends of afghan. Trim fringe evenly.

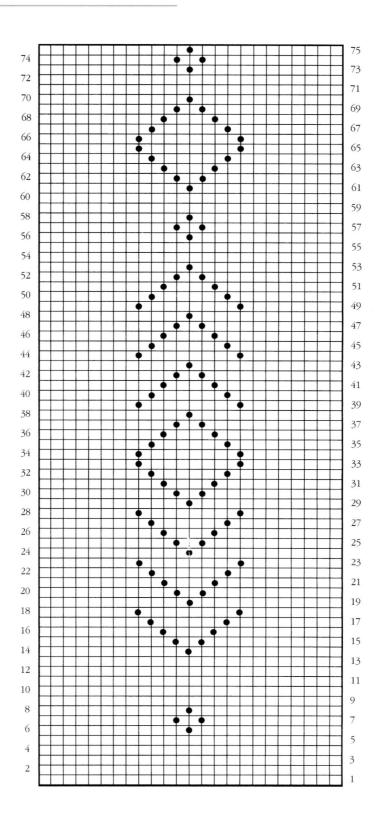

Key

 = Bobble

crochet
Hexagon Wheels

Designed by Nazanin S. Fard

SIZE
56" in diameter

MATERIALS
Worsted weight yarn,
  10½ oz yellow (A)
  10½ oz red (B)
  10½ oz green (C)
  14 oz charcoal grey (D) and
  7 oz white (E)
*Note: Photographed model made with Plymouth Yarn
  Encore #1382 yellow(A), #9601 red(B), #9401 green
  (C), #520 grey(D) and #208 white(E)*
Size G (4mm) crochet hook (or size required
  for gauge)
Piece of cardboard 9" long

GAUGE
16 dc = 4"

Instructions

Hexagons (make 19)

Note: *Each hexagon is formed by joining 6 triangles;
each triangle is formed by joining 3 rings.*

Rings

First Ring

With (A) ch 20, join with a sl st to form a ring.

Rnd 1: Ch 3 (count as a dc), 29 dc in ring: 30 dc;
finish off.

Second Ring

With (B) ch 20; pass the ch through the first ring,
(see Fig), join with a sl st to form a new ring.

Rnd 1: Ch 3, 29 dc in ring: 30 dc; finish off.

Third Ring

With (C) Ch 20; pass the new ch from under both previous rings and bring it over the 2 rings and join with a
sl st to form a ring.

Rnd 1: Ch 3, 29 dc in ring: 30 dc; finish off.

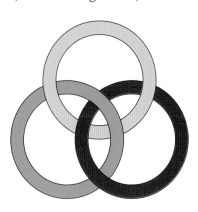

Triangle

Rnd 1: Join (D) to any dc in first ring, ch 3 (counts as
dc), dc in each of next 7 dc on first ring; ch 5, dc in
same st as previous dc, dc in each of 7 dc on first ring;
dc in each of 8 dc on 2nd ring, ch 5, dc in same st as
previous dc; dc in each of 7 dc on 2nd ring; dc in each
of 8 dc on 3rd ring, ch 5, dc in same st as previous dc,
dc in each of 7 dc on 3rd ring; sl st in 3rd ch of beg ch-
3. Finish off.

Joining 6 Triangles

With wrong sides of 2 triangles tog, join (E) in the 3rd
ch of one corner. Insert hook into 3rd ch of the other
triangle, and sc in every ch and sc on one side of the
triangles. Finish off.

Joining Hexagons

With wrong sides tog, join in same manner as joining
triangles, following placement diagram.

Finishing

With (E) work sc around entire outer edge of afghan.
Finish off.

Tassels (make 6):

Step 1: Wrap 1 strand of each color yarn lengthwise
around the cardboard six times.

Wild and wonderful, this afghan made of interlocking circles will appeal to a very special person who appreciates the unusual. The colors add zing to the design.

Step 2: Run a piece of yarn about 9" long through yarn at top of the cardboard, and draw up tightly, knot; leave long yarn ends for sewing to afghan.

Step 3: Cut the bottom edge of yarn and remove the cardboard.

Step 4: Wrap another piece of yarn around all the strands about 1" away from the top. Tie securely and cut end as long as the strands in the tassel.

Step 5: Trim the ends.

Step 6: Securely attach a tassel to every 5th hexagon around outer edge as shown in photo.

Light as a feather, the filet crochet technique is used here to create the dazzling diamonds that dance across this summery afghan. The openwork design is perfect to chase a chill on a warm evening.

crochet
Filet Crochet Lace

Designed by Patons Design Staff

SIZE
56½" x 68"

MATERIALS
Worsted weight yarn,
  46 oz white
Note: *Photographed model made with Patons®*
  Canadiana # 101 Winter White
Size G (4 mm) crochet hook (or size required
  for gauge)

GAUGE
18 dc = 4"

Instructions
Starting at long side edge, ch 319.

Foundation Row: Dc in 5th ch from hook and in each of next 2 chs; (ch 2, skip next 2 chs, dc in next ch) twice; ch 2, skip next 2 chs, dc in each of next 4 chs; *(ch 2, skip next 2 chs, dc in next ch) 10 times; ch 2, skip next 2 chs, dc in each of next 4 chs; rep from * to last 12 chs, (ch 2, skip next 2 chs, dc in next ch) twice; ch 2, skip next 2 chs, dc in each of last 4 chs: 316 sts, counting each ch and beg ch-3 as a st; turn.

Row 1: Ch 6, dc in 5th ch from hook and in next ch, dc in next st; (ch 2, skip next 2 sts, dc in next st) twice; ch 2, skip next 2 sts; (dc in each of next 4 sts, ch 2, skip next 2 sts) twice; *(dc in next st, ch 2, skip next 2 sts) 8 times; (dc in each of next 4 sts, ch 2, skip next 2 sts) twice; rep from * to last 7 sts, (dc in next st, ch 2, skip next 2 sts) twice; (dc, 3 tr) in top of ch 4 at beg of prev row: 322 sts; turn.

Row 2: Ch 6, dc in 5th ch from hook and in next ch, dc in next st; [(ch 2, skip next 2 sts, dc in next st) twice; ch 2, skip next 2 sts, dc in each of next 4 sts] twice; *(ch 2, skip next 2 sts, dc in next st) 6 times; ch 2, skip next 2 sts, dc in each of next 4 sts; (ch 2, skip next 2 sts, dc in next st) twice; ch 2, skip next 2 sts, dc in each of next 4 sts; rep from * to last 9 sts, (ch 2, skip next 2 sts, dc in next st) twice; ch 2, skip next 2 sts, (dc, 3 tr) in top of ch 6 at beg of prev row: 328 sts; turn.

Row 3: Ch 6, dc in 5th ch from hook and in next ch, dc in next st; (ch 2, skip next 2 sts, dc in next st) twice; ch 2, skip next 2 sts, (dc in each of next 4 sts, ch 2, skip next 2 sts) 4 times; *(dc in next st, ch 2, skip next 2 sts) 4 times; (dc in each of next 4 sts, ch 2, skip next 2 sts) 4 times; rep from * to last 7 sts, (dc in next st, ch 2, skip next 2 sts) twice; (dc, 3 tr) in top of ch 6 at beg of prev row: 334 sts; turn.

Row 4: Ch 6, dc in 5th ch from hook and in next ch, dc in next st; (ch 2, skip next 2 sts, dc in next st) twice; ch 2, skip next 2 sts; *dc in each of next 4 sts, (ch 2, skip next 2 sts, dc in next st) twice; ch 2, skip next 2 sts; rep from * to last st, (dc, 3 tr) in top of ch-6 at beg of prev row: 340 sts; turn.

Row 5: Sl st across first 4 sts, ch 3, dc in each of next 3 sts; (ch 2, skip next 2 sts, dc in next st) twice; ch 2, skip next 2 sts, (dc in each of next 4 sts, ch 2, skip next 2 sts) 4 times; *(dc in next st, ch 2, skip next 2 sts) 4 times; (dc in each of next 4 sts, ch 2, skip next 2 sts) 4 times; rep from * to last 13 sts, (dc in next st, ch 2, skip next 2 sts) twice; dc in each of next 4 sts: 334 sts; turn.

Row 6: Sl st across first 4 sts, ch 3, dc in each of next 3 sts; (ch 2, skip next 2 sts, dc in next st) twice; ch 2, skip next 2 sts, dc in each of next 4 sts; (ch 2, skip next 2 sts, dc in next st) twice; ch 2, skip next 2 sts, dc in each of next 4 sts; *(ch 2, skip next 2 sts, dc in next st) 6 times; ch 2, skip next 2 sts, dc in each of next 4 sts; ch 2, skip next 2 sts, dc in next st) twice; ch 2, skip next 2 sts, dc in each of next 4 sts; rep from * to last 15 sts, (ch 2, skip next 2 sts, dc in next st) twice; ch 2, skip next 2 sts, dc in each of next 4 sts: 328 sts; turn.

Row 7: Sl st across first 4 sts, ch 3, dc in each of next 3 sts; (ch 2, skip next 2 sts, dc in next st) twice; ch 2, skip next 2 sts, (dc in each of next 4 sts, ch 2, skip next 2 sts) twice; *(dc in next st, ch 2, skip next 2 sts) 8 times; (dc in each of next 4 sts, ch 2, skip next 2 sts) twice;

rep from* to last 13 sts, (dc in next st, ch 2, skip next 2 sts) twice, dc in each of next 4 sts: 322 sts; turn.

Row 8: Sl st across first 4 sts, ch 3, dc in each of next 3 sts; (ch 2, skip next 2 sts, dc in next st) twice; ch 2, skip next 2 sts, dc in each of next 4 sts; *(ch 2, skip next 2 sts, dc in next st) 10 times; ch 2, skip next 2 sts, dc in each of next 4 sts; rep from * to last 15 sts, (ch 2, skip next 2 sts, dc in next st) twice; ch 2, skip next 2 sts, dc in each of next 4 sts: 316 sts; turn.

Rep Rows 1 through 8 until piece measures about 56½" from beg ch, ending by working a Row 8. Finish off; weave in all ends.

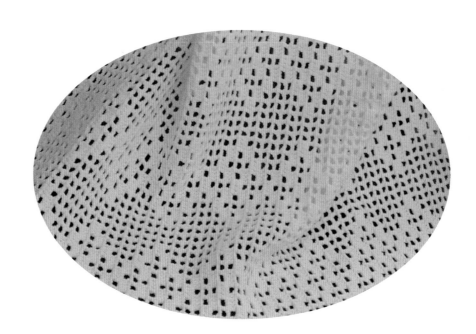

crochet
Rosebuds for a Special Baby

SIZE
35" x 35" including border

MATERIALS
Sport weight yarn,
  20 oz white
*Note: Photographed model made with Red Heart®
  Baby Sport Econo #1 White*
Embroidery floss,
  225 yds dk green
  225 yds dk rose
  225 yds med rose
*Note: Photographed model made with J&P Coats
  Embroidery Floss #6228 dk green, #3500 dk rose
  and #3127 med rose*
Size G (4 mm) crochet hook (or size required
  for gauge)
7/8" wide rose satin ribbon,
  5 yds
5/8" wide rose satin ribbon,
  5 yds
Sewing thread to match ribbon
Sewing needle
Large-eye tapestry needle

GAUGE
15 hdc 15 sts = 3½"
11 hdc rows = 3¼"

STITCH GUIDE

Cluster (CL): (YO, insert hook in specified ch-2 sp and draw up a lp, YO and draw through 2 lps) 3 times, YO and draw through rem 4 lps: CL made.

First Panel (make 5)

First Embroidery Section
Ch 17.

Row 1: Hdc in 3rd ch from hook and in each rem ch: 15 hdc; ch 2, turn. *Note: Do not count turning ch 2 as a st.*

Row 2: Hdc in each hdc, ch 2, turn.

Rows 3 through 12: Rep Row 2; at end of Row 12, do not finish off.

First Pattern Section
Row 1: Hdc in first 2 hdc; *ch 2, skip next hdc, hdc in next hdc; rep from * across, ending with hdc in last hdc, ch 3, turn: 6 ch-2 sps. **Note:** *Mark this row as right side.*

Row 2: Skip first hdc (turning ch-3 counts as first dc) dc in next hdc; *CL (see Stitch Guide) in next ch-2 sp, ch 1, skip next hdc; rep from * across, ending last rep dc in last 2 hdc; ch 2, turn.

Row 3: Hdc in first 2 dc; *ch 2, skip next CL, hdc in next ch-1 sp; rep from * across, working hdc of last rep in next dc instead of ch-1, hdc in top of ch-3; ch 3, turn.

Rep Rows 2 and 3 three times more. At end of last Row 3, ch 2, turn.

Second Embroidery Section
Row 1: Hdc in first 2 hdc; *hdc in next ch-2 sp, hdc in next hdc; rep from * across, ending with hdc in last hdc: 15 hdc; ch 2, turn.

Row 2: Hdc in each hdc, ch 2, turn.

Rep Row 2 nine times more.

Rep First Pattern Section and Second Embroidered Section 3 times more: 9 alternating sections completed.

At end of last row, rep Row 2 of Embroidered Section. Do not ch 2, turn. Finish off. Weave in all ends.

Second Panel (make 4)

First Pattern Section
Ch 17.

Foundation Row: Hdc in 3rd ch from hook and in each rem ch: 15 hdc; ch 2, turn. Do not count ch-2 as a

Every mother will love the rosebuds and ribbons that accent this magnificent afghan to be created for a cherished baby. The Victorian style has a timeless quality.

st. Complete as for Pattern Section on First Panel.

Embroiderey Section

Work as for Second Embroidery Section of First Panel.

Second Pattern Section

Work as for Pattern Section of First Panel.

Rep Embroidery and Second Pattern Sections 3 times more: 9 alternating sections completed. At end of last row, rep Row 1 of Second Embroidery Section. Do not ch 2, turn. Finish off. Weave in all ends.

Joining Panels

Holding right sides tog and alternating panels so that a First Panel is on each outer side edge, sl st panels tog, making sure embroidey and pattern sections are opposite each other.

Border

Rnd 1: With right side facing, attach yarn in corner st in upper right corner, ch 3 (counts as a dc), 4 dc in same st: beg corner made; * work 115 dc evenly spaced across edge to next corner st, 5 dc in corner st: corner made; work 126 dc evenly spaced across next edge to next corner st, work 5 dc in corner st; rep from * around, join with sl st in top of beg ch-3.

Rnd 2: Ch 6 (counts a tr and a ch-2 sp), skip next 2 dc; * tr in next dc, ch 2, skip next 2 dc: tr-block made; work tr-blocks across to 3rd dc of next 5-dc corner group; tr in 3rd dc, ch 5 and tr in 3rd dc: corner tr-block made; ch 2, skip next 2 dc; rep from * around, sl st in 4th ch of beg ch-6.

Rnd 3: Ch 5 (counts as a dc and a ch-2 sp), skip next ch-2 sp; *dc in next tr, ch 2, skip next ch-2 sp: dc-block made; work dc-blocks across to 3rd ch of corner ch-5; (dc, ch 5 and dc) in 3rd ch, ch 2, skip next ch-2 sp; rep from * around, sl st in 3rd ch of beg ch-5.

Rnd 4: Ch 1, sc in same st as joining; *(sl st, sc) in next ch-2 sp, sc in next dc; rep from * across to next ch-5 corner sp; (sl st, sc, sl st) over first 2 chs of corner sp, 3 sc in 3rd ch of ch-5; (sl st, sc and sl st) over 4th and 5th chs of corner sp, sc in next dc: corner section made; rep from first * around, end sl st in beg sc; finish off.

Rnd 5: With wrong side facing, attach yarn with sl st in 2nd sc of any 3-sc corner group; in same st work (sl st, tr, sl st, sc, sl st, tr, sl st): 2-bobble corner group made; sc in next sc; *sl st in next sl st, tr in next sc, sl st in next sl st, sc in next sc: sl st pat established; work sl st pat across to 2nd sc of next 3-sc corner group **; work 2-bobble corner group in 2nd sc, sc in next sc; rep from * around, end last rep at **; join in beg sl st; finish off.

Rnd 6: With right side facing, attach yarn to sc following any 2-bobble corner group, ch 5 (counts as a dc and a ch-2 sp), skip next sl st, tr and sl st; *dc in next sc, ch 2, skip next sl st, tr and sl st: dc-block made; work dc-blocks across to corner sc of next 2-bobble corner group; (dc, ch 5, dc) in corner sc, ch 2, skip next sl st, tr and sl st; rep from * around; join in 3rd ch of beg ch-5.

Rnds 7 and 8: Rep Rnds 4 and 5. Finish off, weave in ends.

Embroidery

Following diagram, work one flower centered in each Embroidery Section of each panel. Work with 12 strands of thread in needle, using straight sts for stem and flower, Lazy Daisy st for leaves and French knots for flower center.

Insert Ribbon

Weave 7/8" ribbon under and over trs of Border Rnd 2 as shown in photo; turn under cut ends and sew together. Tack corners in place with matching sewing thread.

Rep with 5/8" ribbon, weaving through Rnd 3.

See Embroidery Stitches on page 114

Embroidery Stitches

Straight Stitch

This is shown as single spaced stitches worked either in a regular or irregular manner. Sometimes the stitches are of varying size. The stitches should be neither too long or too loose.

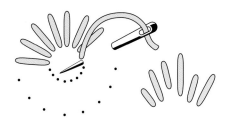

Lazy Daisy Stitch

Bring thread up, hold down with left thumb. Insert needle where it last emerged and bring the point out a short distance away (A). Fasten each loop at center with a small stitch (B)

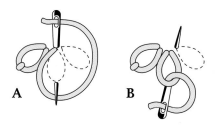

French Knots

Bring thread up, hold down with left thumb and wind thread twice around the needle (A). Still holding thread firmly, twist the needle back to the starting point and insert it close to where the thread first emerged (see arrow). Pull thread through to back and pass on to the next stitch (B).

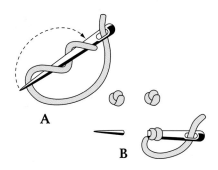

Full-Size Diagram for Embroidery

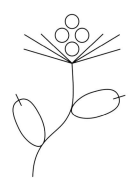

114

Cabin in the Woods

Designed by Linda Taylor

SIZE
52" x 72" before edging

MATERIALS
Worsted weight yarn,
   21 oz red (A);
   14 oz white (B)
   14 oz lt grey (C)
   14 oz dk grey (D)
   14 oz black (E)
Note: Photographed model made with Unger Utopia, #236 Red (A); #200 White (B), #71 Soft Grey (C), #103 Pewter (D) and # 104 Black (E)
Size I (5.5 mm) crochet hook (or size required for gauge)

GAUGE
5 shells = 3"
1 block = 12" x 13"

STITCH GUIDE

Shell: (Sc, ch 2, sc) in specified ch or ch-2 sp

Instructions

Note: Afghan is made up of 24 blocks; each block has 13 "patches". Instructions for all blocks are the same, only colors are different.

Block A (make 6)

First (center) Patch

With Color A, loosely ch 12.

Row 1: Working in back bumps of each ch, shell in 2nd ch from hook, (skip next ch, shell in next ch) 5 times: 6 shells made; ch 1, turn.

Rows 2 through 13: Shell in ch-2 sp of each shell, ch 1, turn. Mark last row as right side; finish off Color A.

Second Patch

Turn work so yarn tail from last completed row is on top and to the right. Attach Color B in ch-2 of first shell with a sl st, ch 1.

Rows 1 through 4: Shell in ch-2 sp of each shell, ch 1, turn. At end of Row 4, finish off Color B. With Second Patch on top and with right side facing, rotate work one turn to the right so Color B is on the right. Next row is worked along the end of Second Patch and side of First Patch.

Third Patch

Attach Color C with a sl st in st to the right of the rightmost "bump" created by sts on the turning ends of the patch, ch 1.

Row 1: Working in sts at turning ends of each previous patch, work 8 shells across, ch 1, turn.

Rows 2 through 4: Shell in each shell, ch 1, turn. At end of last row, finish off C; turn piece back to right side.

Fourth Patch

With third patch on top and right side facing, turn work one turn to the right so third patch is to the right. Now work along the bottoms of Third and First Patch.

Row 1: Attach Color D the same way you attached Color C. The first 2 shell sts are worked exactly as for Color C, but the next 6 are worked in the "holes" created by the first row of Color A; ch 1, turn: 8 shell sts.

Rows 2 through 4: Shell in shell, ch 1, turn. At end of last row, finish off, turn work to right side.

Fifth Patch

With Fourth patch on top, rotate work one turn to the right so Color D is on your right.

Row 1: Attach Color E and work 10 shells across; sl st into side of last st of Color B to anchor; ch 1, turn.

The traditional Log Cabin quilt pattern is beautifully rendered in crochet in this nostalgic afghan. You can almost see the homesteader sitting at her wheel spinning fiber to warm her family in their cozy little home nestled in the woods.

Rows 2 through 4: Shell in shell, ch 1, turn; at end of last row, finish off, turn work to right side.

Continue in this manner for Sixth through Thirteenth patches, following patch placement as show in **Fig 1** and in following color sequence:
Sixth Patch, C; Seventh Patch, D; Eighth Patch, E; Ninth Patch, B; Tenth Patch, D; Eleventh Patch, E; Twelfth Patch, B; Thirteenth Patch, C.

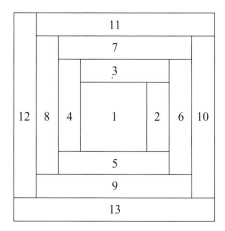

Fig 1

Edging

Rnd 1: Hold Block with right side facing; join A in any outer corner, ch 1, (shell, ch 2, shell) in same st for corner; work shell pattern around entire outer edge of Block, working (shell, ch 2, shell) shells in each corner; join.

Rnd 2: Sc around, working 2 sc in each-ch 2 sp, adjusting sts as needed to keep work flat; join, finish off; weave in all ends.

Block B (make 6)

Work as Block A in following color sequence:
First Patch, A; Second Patch, C; Third Patch, D; Fourth Patch, E; Fifth Patch, B; Sixth Patch D; Seventh Patch, E; Eighth Patch B; Ninth Patch, C; Tenth Patch, E; Eleventh Patch, B; Twelfth Patch, C; Thirteenth Patch, D. With A, work Edging.

Block C (make 6)

Work as Block A in following color sequence:
First Patch, A; Second Patch, D; Third Patch, E; Fourth Patch B; Fifth Patch, C; Sixth Patch, E; Seventh Patch, B; Eighth Patch C; Ninth Patch, D; Tenth Patch, B; Eleventh Patch, C; Twelfth Patch D, Thirteenth Patch, E. With A, work Edging.

Block D (make 6)

Work as Block A in following color sequence: First Patch, A; Second Patch, E; Third Patch B; Fourth Patch, C; Fifth Patch, E; Sixth Patch, B; Seventh Patch C; Eighth Patch D; Ninth Patch E; Tenth Patch, C; Eleventh Patch, D; Twelfth Patch E; Thirteenth Patch, B. With A, work Edging.

Joining

Join blocks in 6 rows of 4 squares each being sure long length of each block runs top to bottom, following this color sequence from left to right across rows:

Row 1: Blocks A, B, C D.

Row 2: Blocks B, C, D, A.

Row 3: Blocks C, D, A, B.

Row 4: Blocks D, A, B, C.

Row 5: Blocks A, B, C, D

Row 6: Blocks B, C, D, A

To join, place two blocks side by side and with red, carefully matching sts, sl st in one square, then in matching st on opposite squaare.

Join into rows in same manner, then join rows.

Edging

Rnd 1: Hold afghan with right side facing; join A in upper right outer corner, ch 1, 3 sc in same place; sc evenly around, adjusting sts to keep work flat and working 3 sc in each corner; join,

Rnd 2: Ch 1, work shell pattern around, working a shell in every 3rd sc and a shell in center sc of each 3-sc corner group of Rnd 1, join, finish off.

This enchanting afghan can be used to warm the little one, or as a colorful focal point on the wall of the nursery. It has the look of a vintage sampler, complete with alphabet letters and playful motifs: a cat and mouse, elephants, ducks, fish, and birds on the wing.

Baby's First Sampler

Designed by Julia Bryant

SIZE
27" x 36"

MATERIALS
Sport weight yarn,
  16 oz off white
  2 oz red
Tapestry or needlepoint yarn,
  small quantities of royal blue, pale blue,
  medium pink, yellow, purple, brown, turquoise,
  dark grey, black, orange, lilac, ginger.
Size G (4 mm) afghan crochet hook (or size required
  for gauge)
Size E (3.5 mm) crochet hook

GAUGE
6 sts =1" in afghan st
5 rows =1" in afghan st

*Note: This afghan can be worked either with the design
worked in from the chart as you go, or the design can be
worked in later in cross stitch, on the completed square,
using the same chart.*

STITCH GUIDE

Afghan Stitch: Follow instructions on page 124.

Cross Stitch on Afghan Stitch: Follow instructions
on page 124.

Bobble (BB): YO, insert hook in next vertical st and
pull up a lp; YO, insert hook in same vertical st and
pull up a lp (4 lps now on hook); YO and pull through
all 4 lps, ch 1: BB made. Note: the completed BB will
appear on the row below.

Instructions

Method 1 (worked-in designs)

Squares (make 12 different)
Ch 49.

Work 41 rows in afghan st following charts starting on
page 98 and using colors indicated; Work in bobbles as
indicated on charts.

Method 2 (cross stitch designs)

Squares (make 12 alike)
Ch 49.

Work 41 rows in afghan stitch following any of the
charts starting on page 98, working bobbles as indicated on chart and omitting design.

Finishing

Block each square, and steam lightly using a damp
cloth. Allow to dry completely.

To join, hold 2 squares with right sides facing and
join with sc with crochet hook, carefully matching sts
and corners. Join in 4 rows of 3 squares each as shown
in photo.

Border

Hold piece with right side facing and join off white
with crochet hook in upper right corner.

Rnd 1: Ch 1, 3 sc in same st for corner; sc in each st
and row around, working 3 sc in each corner, and
adjusting sts as need to keep work flat; join with sl st
in beg sc.

Rnd 2: * Sc in next 3 sts, ch 3, sl st in first ch worked:
picot made; rep from * around, join with sl st in beg sc;
finish off, weave in ends.

Baby's First Sampler

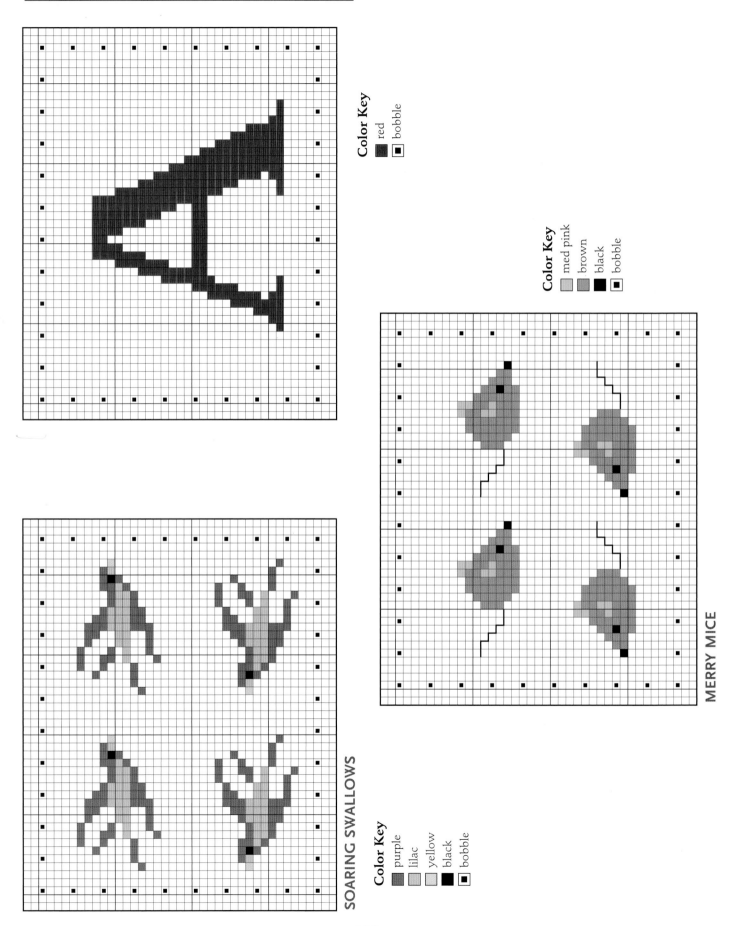

Color Key
- ■ red
- ▣ bobble

Color Key
- med pink
- brown
- black
- bobble

MERRY MICE

Color Key
- purple
- lilac
- yellow
- black
- bobble

SOARING SWALLOWS

120

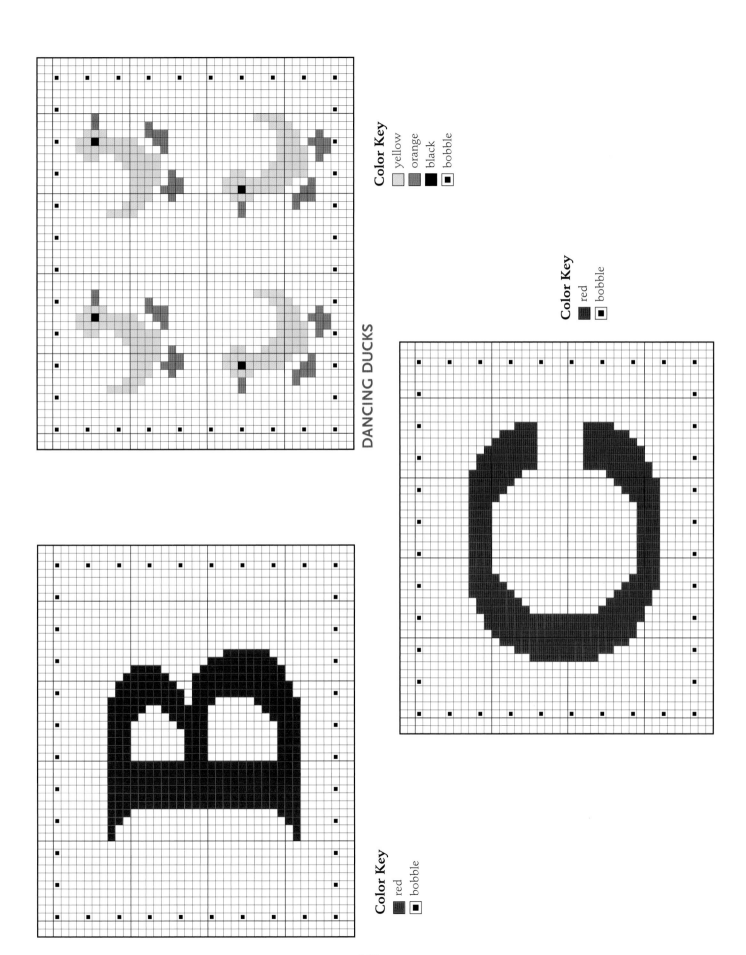

DANCING DUCKS

Color Key
- yellow
- orange
- black
- bobble

Color Key
- red
- bobble

Color Key
- red
- bobble

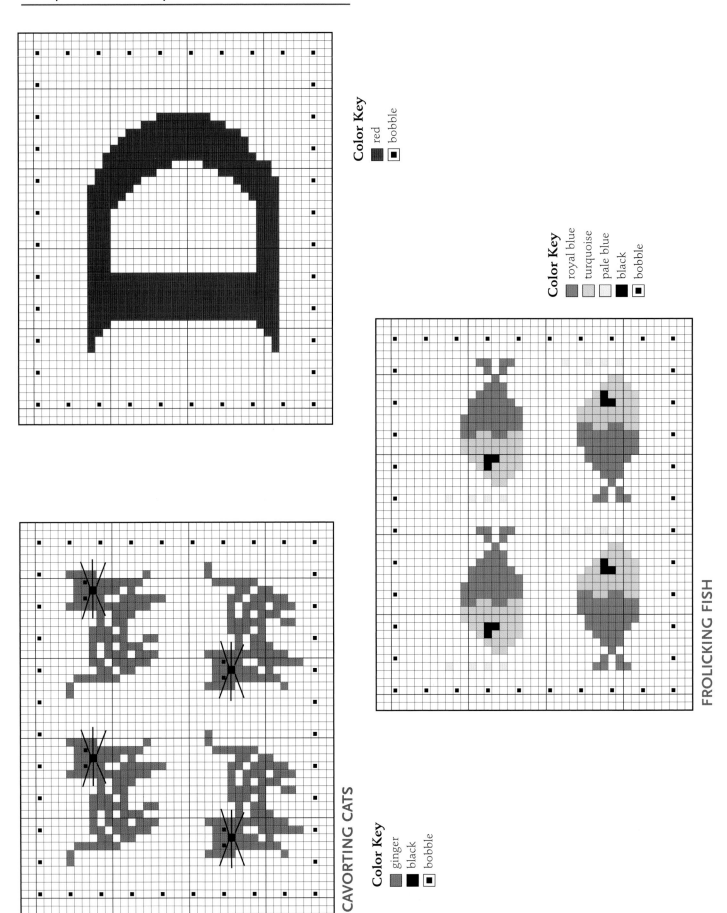

Color Key
■ red
□■ bobble

Color Key
■ royal blue
■ turquoise
□ pale blue
■ black
□■ bobble

FROLICKING FISH

CAVORTING CATS

Color Key
■ ginger
■ black
□■ bobble

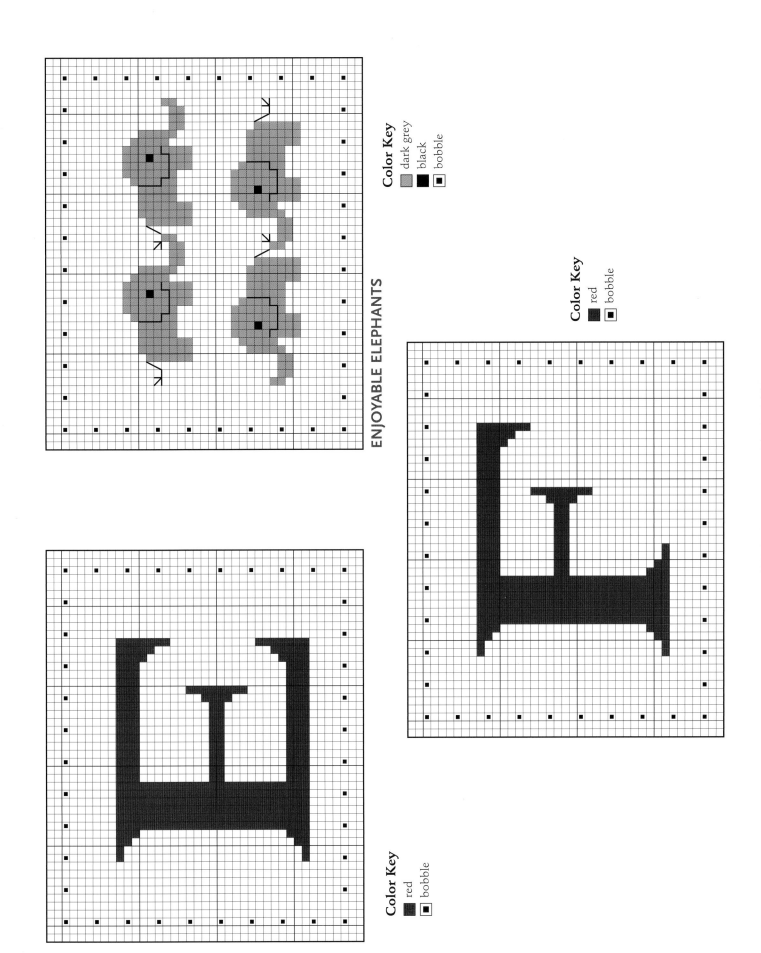

ENJOYABLE ELEPHANTS

Color Key
- ▨ dark grey
- ■ black
- ⬚ bobble

Color Key
- ■ red
- ⬚ bobble

Color Key
- ■ red
- ⬚ bobble

123

General Directions

Basic Afghan Stitch

Ch loosely the number specified in the pattern instructions.

1. Insert hook into 2nd ch from hook. YO and draw lp through. Leave on hook.

2. *Insert hook into next ch. YO and draw lp through. Leave on hook; rep from * to end of chain.

3. YO and draw through one lp.

4. and 5. *YO and draw through 2 lps; rep from * until one lp remains on hook. (First row of basic afghan stitch is complete.)

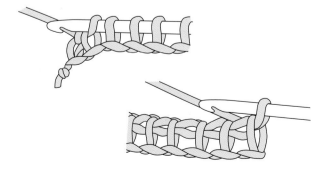

6. For subsequent rows, insert hook from right to left under single vertical strand from each st of previous row beginning in 2nd strand. YO and draw lp through. Leave on hook; rep to end. Complete rem of row as show in diagrams 3 to 5.

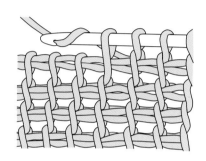

Cross Stitch on Afghan Stitch

Cross stitch on afghan stitch is worked from a chart with a key to the colors used. Each square on the chart represents one bar. One cross stitch is worked over one vertical bar.

To work cross stitch, thread tapestry needle with desired length of yarn. Count over required number of bars to where you wish to begin. Bring yarn through from back of work to front, leaving a 1" end to be worked over (do not knot). Work cross stitches, being careful not to pull stitches too tightly. Be sure that the top cross of each stitch lies in the same direction. Do not make knots; weave in all ends through sts on back of afghan.

Abbreviations and Symbols

Knit and crochet patterns are written in a special shorthand, which is used so that instructions don't take up too much space. They sometimes seem confusing, but once you learn them, you'll have no trouble following them.

These are Standard Abbreviations

BB . . . . bobble
Beg . . . . beginning
BLO . . . . back loop only
BO . . . . bind off
BPdc . . . . . . Back post double crochet
CL(s) . . . . cluster(s)
CO . . . . cast on
Cont . . . . continue
Ch(s) . . . . chain(s)
Dc . . . . double crochet
Dc2tog . . . . Double crochet
          2 sts together decrease
Dec . . . . decrease
Dtr . . . . double triple crochet
Fig. . . . . figure
FPdc. . . . . . . front post double crochet
FPdtr . . front post double triple crochet
FPtr. . . . . front post triple crochet
G . . . . gram(s)
Hdc . . . . half double crochet
Inc . . . . increase(ing)
K . . . . knit
Lp(s) . . . . loop(s)
M1 . . . . Increase one stitch
Mm. . . . . millimeter(s)
Oz . . . . ounces
P. . . . . purl
Pat(t). pattern
PC . . . . popcorn
Prev . . . . previous
PSSO . . . . pass the slipped stitch over
P2SSO . . . pass 2 slipped stitches over
Pst. puff stitch
Rem . . . . remain(ing)
Rep. . . . . repeat(ing)

Rev Sc . . . . reverse single crochet
Rnd(s). . . . . round(s)
Sc . . . . single crochet
Sc dec . . . . . . single crochet decrease
Sc2tog. . . . . single crochet
          2 stitches together decrease
Sc3tog. . . . . single crochet
          3 stitches together decrease
Sk . . . . skip
Sl. . . . . slip
Sp(s) . . . . space(s)
SSK . . . . slip, slip, knit
SSP. . . . . slip, slip, purl
St(s) . . . . stitch(es)
Stock st. . . . . stockinette stitch
Tbl . . . . through back loop
Tog. . . . . together
Tr. . . . . triple crochet
Trtr. . . . . triple triple crochet
YB . . . yarn in back of needle or hook
YF . . . yarn in front of needle or hook
YO . . . . Yarn over the needle or hook
YRN . . . . Yarn around needle

These are Standard Symbols

*An asterisk (or double asterisks**) in a pattern row, indicates a portion of instructions to be used more than once. For instance, "rep from * three times" means that after working the instructions once, you must work them again three times for a total of 4 times in all.

† A dagger (or double daggers ††) indicates that those instructions will be repeated again later in the same row or round.

: The number after a colon tells you the number of stitches you will have when you have completed the row or round.

( ) Parentheses enclose instructions which are to be worked the number of times following the parentheses.

For instance, "(ch1, sc, ch1) 3 times" means that you will chain one, work one sc, and then chain again three times for a total of six chains and 3cs, or "(K1, P2) 3 times" means that you knit one stitch and then purl two stitches, three times.

Parentheses often set off or clarify a group of stitches to be worked into the same space or stitch. For instance, "(dc, ch2, dc) in corner sp."

[ ] Brackets and ( ) parentheses are also used to give you additional information.

TERMS

Front Loop—This is the loop toward you at the top of the crochet stitch.

Back Loop—This is the loop away from you at the top of the crochet stitch.

Post—This is the vertical part of the crochet stitch

Join—This means to join with a sl st unless another stitch is specified.

Finish off—This means to end your piece by pulling the yarn through the last loop remaining on the hook or needle. This will prevent the work from unraveling.

Continue in Pattern as Established—This means to follow the pattern stitch as it has been set up, working any increases or decreases in such a way that the pattern remains the same as it was established.

Work even—This means that the work is continued in the pattern as established without increasing or decreasing.

Right Side—This means the side of the afghan that will be seen.

Wrong Side—This means the side of the afghan that will not be seen.

Gauge

This is probably the most important aspect of knitting and crocheting!

GAUGE simply means the number of stitches per inch, and the numbers of rows per inch that result from a specified yarn worked with hooks or needles in a specified size. But since everyone knits or crochets differently—some loosely, some tightly, some in-between—the measurements of individual work can vary greatly, even when the crocheters or knitters use the same pattern and the same size yarn and hook or needle.

If you don't work to the gauge specified in the pattern, your afghan will never be the correct size, and you may not have enough yarn to finish your project. Hook and needle sizes given in instructions are merely guides, and should never be used without a gauge swatch.

To make a gauge swatch, crochet or knit a swatch that is about 4" square, using the suggested hook or needle and the number of stitches given in the pattern. Measure your swatch. If the number of stitches is fewer than those listed in the pattern, try making another swatch with a smaller hook or needle. If the number of stitches is more than is called for in the pattern, try making another swatch with a larger hook or needle. It is your responsibility to make sure you achieve the gauge specified in the pattern.

The patterns in this book have been written using the knitting and crochet terminology that is used in the United States. Terms which may have different equivalents in other parts of the world are listed below.

United States	International
Double crochet (dc)	treble crochet (tr)
Gauge	tension
Half double crochet (hdc)	half treble crochet (htr)
Single crochet	double crochet
Skip	miss
Slip stitch	single crochet
Triple crochet (tr)	double treble crochet (dtr)
Yarn over (YO)	yarn forward (yfwd)
Yarn around needle (yrn)	yarn over hook (yoh)

Knitting Needles Conversion Chart

U.S.	0	1	2	3	4	5	6	7	8	9	10	10½	11	13	15	17
Metric	2	2.25	2.75	3.25	3.5	3.75	4	4.5	5	5.5	6	6.5	8	9	10	12.75

Crochet Hooks Conversion Chart

U.S.	B-1	C-2	D-3	E-4	F-5	G-6	H-8	I-9	J-10	K-10 12	N	P	Q
Metric	2.25	2.75	3.25	3.5	3.75	4	5	5.5	6	6.5	0	10	15

Steel Crochet Hooks Conversion Chart

U.S.	00	0	1	2	3	4	5	6	7	8	9	10	11	12	13	14
Metric	3.5	3.25	2.75	2.25	2.1	2	1.9	1.8	1.65	1.5	1.4	1.3	1.1	1.0	0.85	0.75

Fringe

Basic Instructions

Cut a piece of cardboard about 6" wide and half as long as specified in the instructions for strands, plus ½" for trimming allowance. Wind the yarn loosely and evenly lengthwise around the cardboard. When the card is filled, cut the yarn across one end. Do this several times; then begin fringing. You can wind additional strands as you need them.

Single Knot Fringe

Hold the specified number of strands for one knot of fringe together, then fold in half.

Hold the project with the right side facing you. Using a crochet hook, draw the folded ends through the space or stitch from right to wrong side.

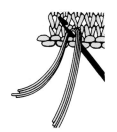 

Pull the loose ends through the folded section.

Draw the knot up firmly.

Space the knots evenly and trim the ends of the fringe.

Double Knot Fringe

Begin by working Single Knot Fringe. With right side facing you and working from left to right, take half the strands of one knot and half the strands in the knot next to it, and knot them together.

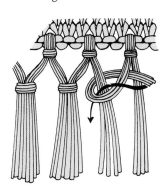

Triple Knot Fringe

First work Double Knot Fringe. Then working again on right side from left to right, tie the third row of knots.

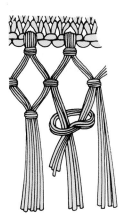

Index